CW00547347

North Coast 500

CONTENTS

Reference / legend 2-3

Key to map pages 4-5

Map pages 6-99

Index 100-109

Route planner 110-115

Safety & Security 116-118

Notes 119-120

Published by Geographers' A-Z Map Company Limited
An imprint of HarperCollins Publishers
Westerhill Road
Bishopbriggs
Glasgow
G64 2QT

www.az.co.uk
a-z.maps@harpercollins.co.uk

HarperCollins Publishers
Macken House, 39/40 Mayor Street Upper
Dublin 1, D01 C9W8, Ireland

1st edition 2024

© HarperCollins Publishers Ltd 2024. Published in association with North Coast 500 Ltd.
Maps © Collins Bartholomew 2024

Map data © OpenStreetMap contributors
Contains OS data © Crown copyright and database rights (2024)

AZ, A-Z and AtoZ are registered trademarks of Geographers' A-Z Map Company Limited

NC500 © and North Coast 500 © are registered trademarks of North Coast 500 Ltd.

Electric charge point data from Zapmap.

Cover image: Loch Maree viewpoint (Shutterstock / LouieLea)
Inside front cover image: Kylesku Bridge on the A894 (Shutterstock / David W Bird)

Every care has been taken in the preparation of this guide. However, the Publisher accepts no responsibility whatsoever for any loss, damage, injury or inconvenience sustained or caused as a result of using this map. The representation of a road, track or footpath is no evidence of a right of way.

A catalogue record for this book is available from the British Library.

ISBN 978-0-00-866063-5

10 9 8 7 6 5 4 3 2 1

Printed in India

MIX
Paper | Supporting responsible forestry
FSC™ C007454

GENERAL KEY

M90	Motorway
A836	Primary road (dual/single carriageway)
B869	B road
	Minor road
	Other road
	Track
	Path
	National Cycle Network
Beauly	Railway / station
	North Coast 500
515	Route points at 5 mile intervals
	Core path
	Woodland
	Built up area
	Lake / river
	Mud / sand
	Cliffs
	Rocks
70	Contour with height (in metres)
102°	Summit with height (in metres)
▲	Youth hostel
	Lighthouse

Rights of way are liable to change and may not be clearly defined on the ground.
Please check with the relevant local authority for the latest information.
The representation on this map of any other road, track or path is no evidence of a right of way.
Alignments are based on the best information available.

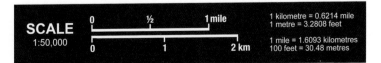

SCALE
1:50,000

0	½	1 mile	1 kilometre = 0.6214 mile
			1 metre = 3.2808 feet
0	1	2 km	1 mile = 1.6093 kilometres
			100 feet = 30.48 metres

TOURIST & LEISURE KEY

🏛	Art gallery
🏚	Building of historic interest
⌂	Camping and caravan site
🚐	Caravan site
🏰	Castle or fort
✝	Cathedral or abbey
⚘	Craft centre
🔋	Electric charge point
✿	Garden or arboretum
⚑	Golf course
HC	Heritage centre
i	Information centre
🏛	Museum
✾	National Trust for Scotland
🐦	Nature reserve
☆	Other tourist feature
⊗	Outdoor recreation
⛽	Petrol station
☀	Viewpoint
V	Visitor centre
🏄	Water activities (board)

Locations of charge points and petrol stations are liable to change.
Please check with the relevant provider for the latest information.

KEY TO MAP PAGES

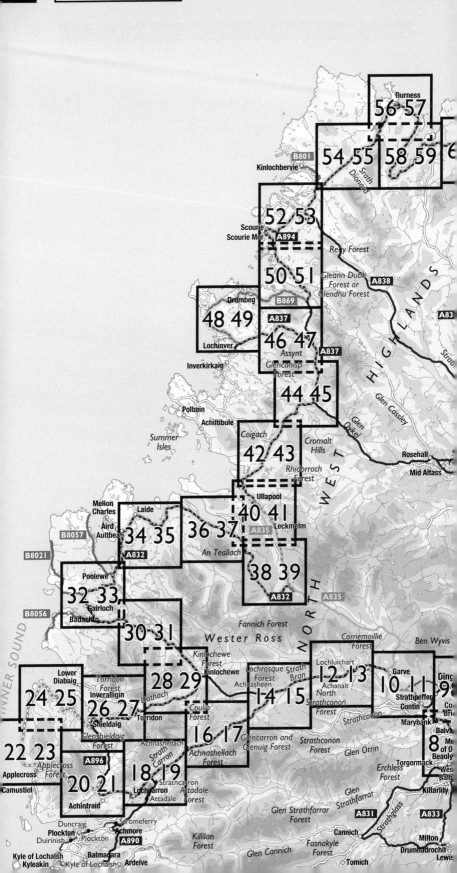

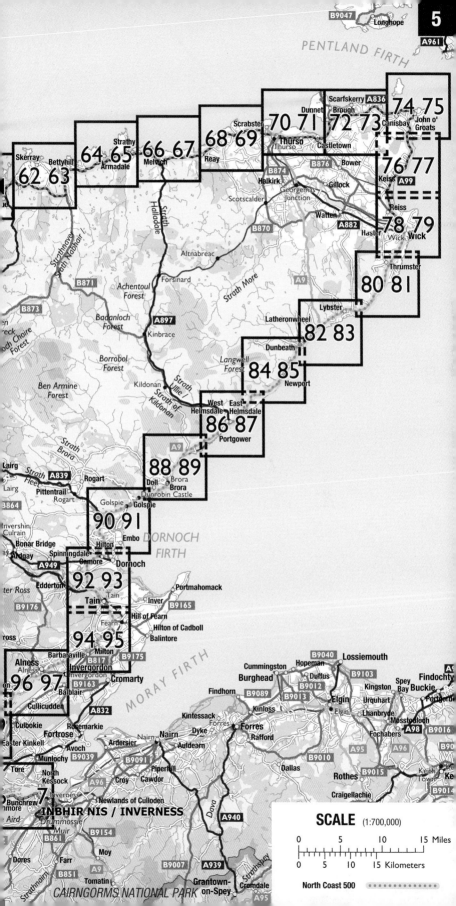

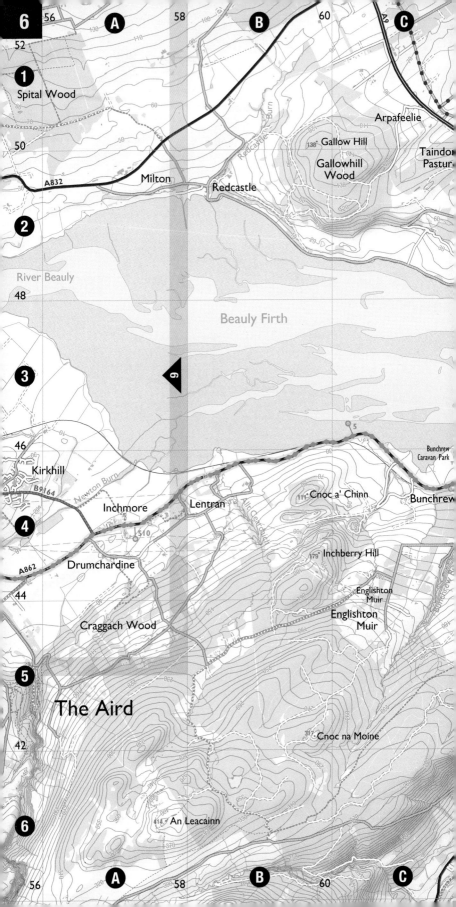

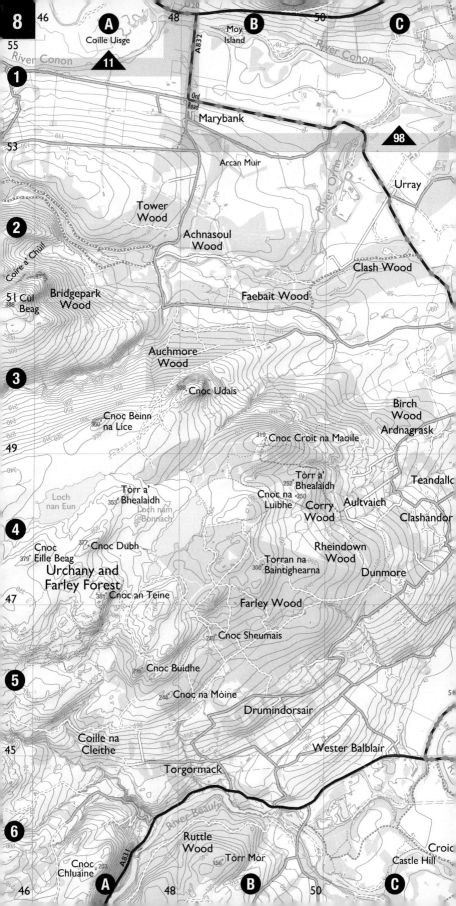

8 46

A 48 **B** 50 **C**

55

Coille Uisge

River Conon

▲11

Moy Island

River Conon

1

Ord Road

A832

Marybank

▲98

53

Arcan Muir

River Orrin

Urray

Tower Wood

Achnasoul Wood

Coire a' Chùil

2

Clash Wood

51 Cùl Beag

Bridgepark Wood

Faebait Wood

Auchmore Wood

3

Cnoc Udais

Birch Wood

Ardnagrask

Cnoc Beinn na Lice

Cnoc Croit na Maoile

49

Tòrr a' Bhealaidh

Teandallo

Loch nan Eun

Tòrr a' Bhealaidh

Cnoc na Luibhe

Corry Wood

Aultvaich

Loch nam Bonnach

Clashandor

4

Cnoc Eille Beag

Cnoc Dubh

Rheindown Wood

Dunmore

Urchany and Farley Forest

Torran na Baintighearna

47

Cnoc an Teine

Farley Wood

Cnoc Sheumais

Cnoc Buidhe

5

Cnoc na Mòine

Drumindorsair

45

Coille na Cleithe

Wester Balblair

Torgormack

River Beauly

6

Ruttle Wood

Croic

A831

Cnoc Chluaine

Tòrr Mòr

Castle Hill

46

A 48 **B** 50 **C**

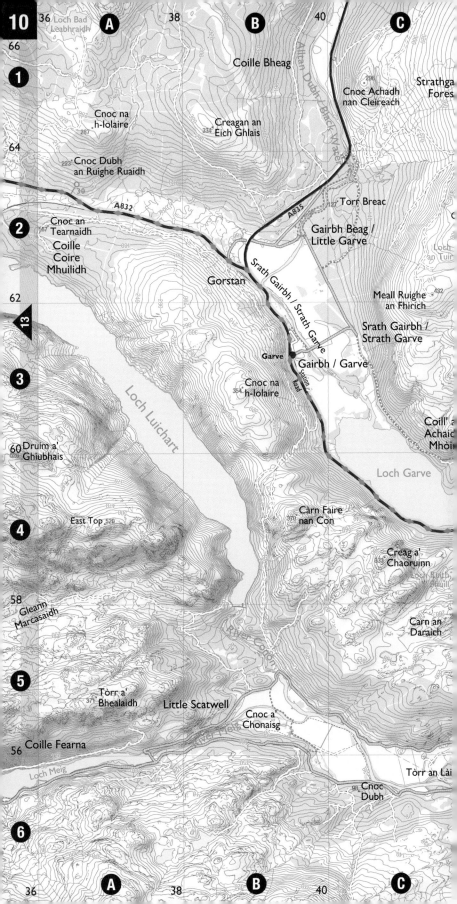

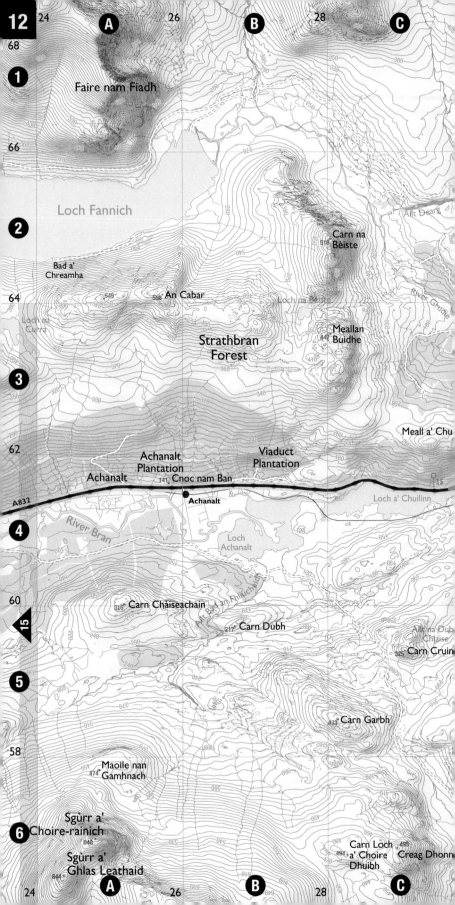

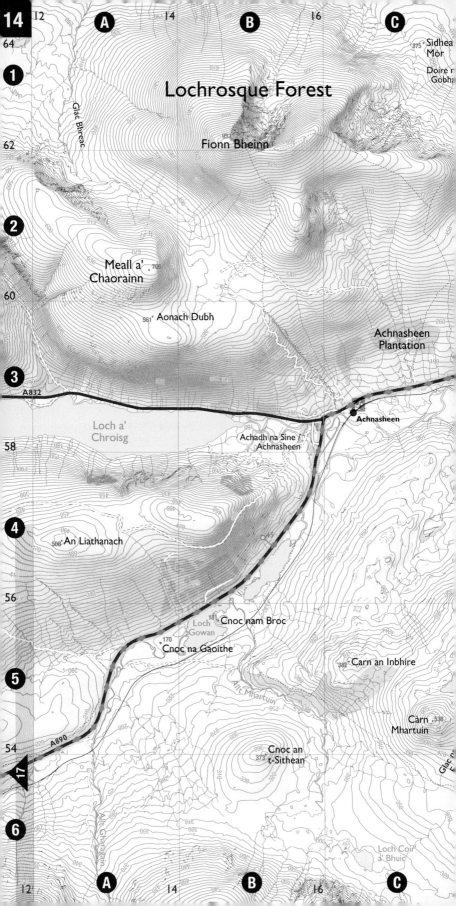

Loch na Mòine Mòr

Loch na Curra

64

Meallan Odhar

Carn Daraich

Glac Mhòr a' Chairn-daraich

Loch na Mòine Beag

Loch Dail Fhearna

62

Glac a' Mhuchaidh

Rosebank Plantation

Strathbran Plantation

Cnoc Bàn

Dos Mhucarain

40

Strath Bran

60

Dosmucheran Plantation

River Bran

A832

58

Carn na Fèith-Rabhain

North Strathconon Forest

Sgùrr a' Ghlas Leathaid

56

Càrn artuin

Càrn a' Chaorainn

Gleann Meinich

54

Cnap na Feola

Carn an Leanaidh

Coire Dubh

Bràigh na Leitire

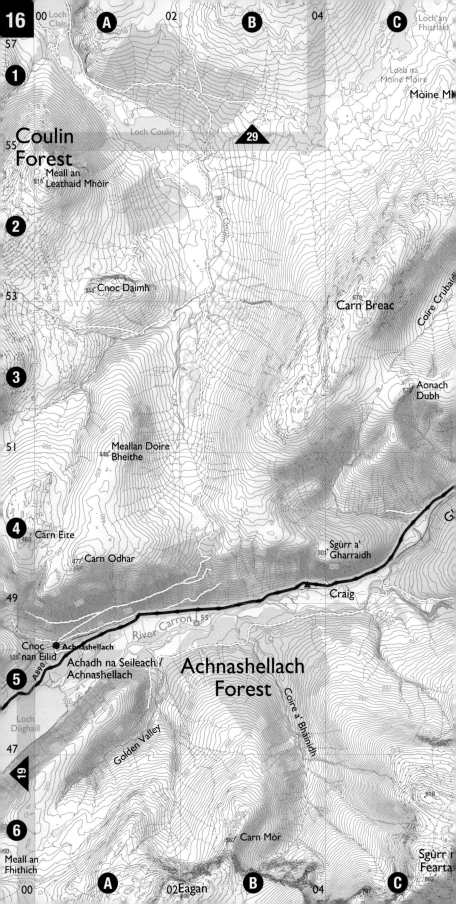

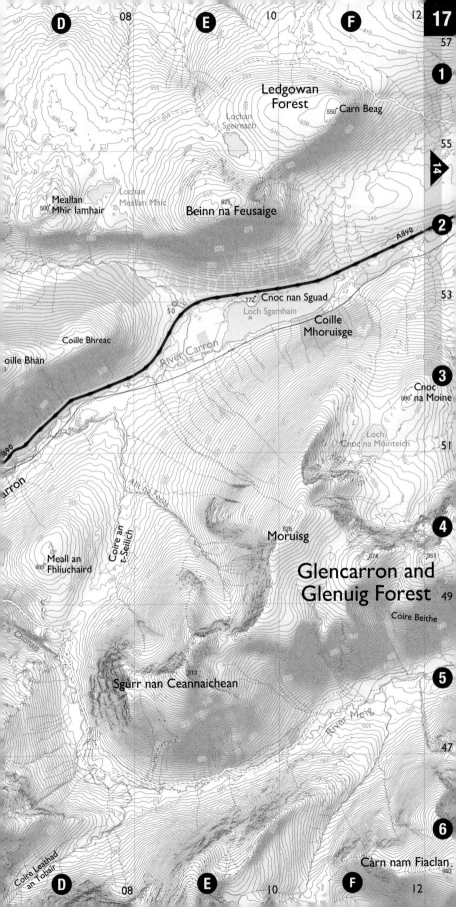

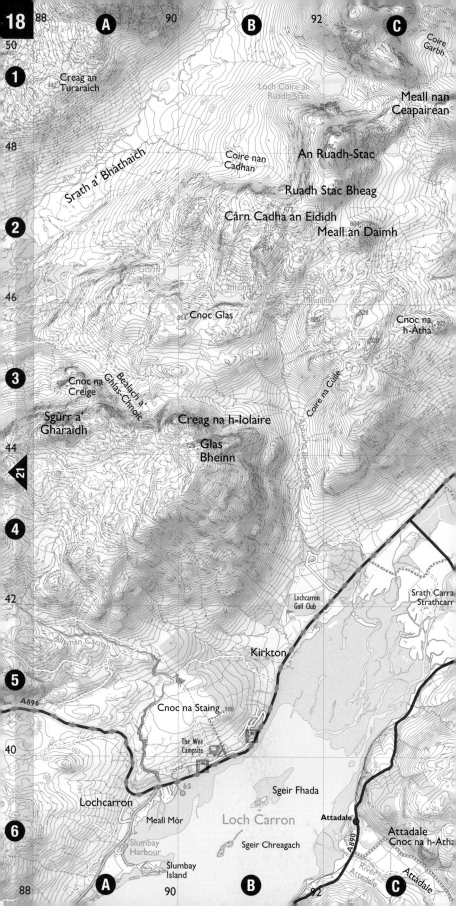

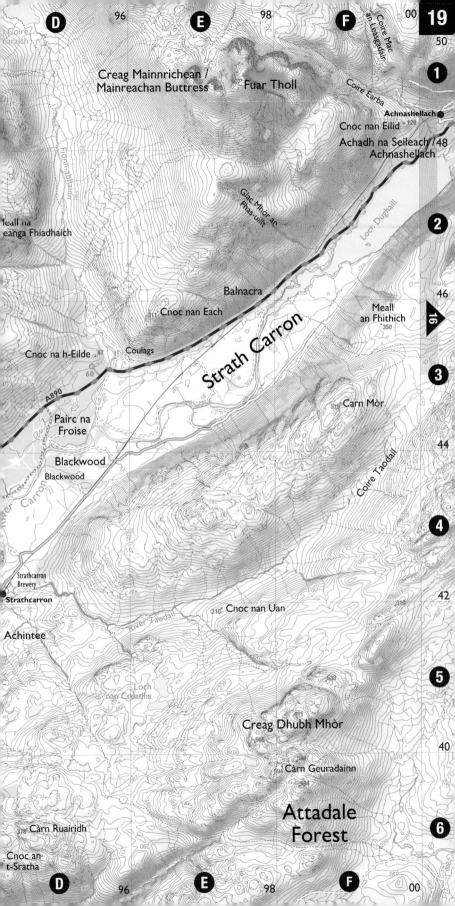

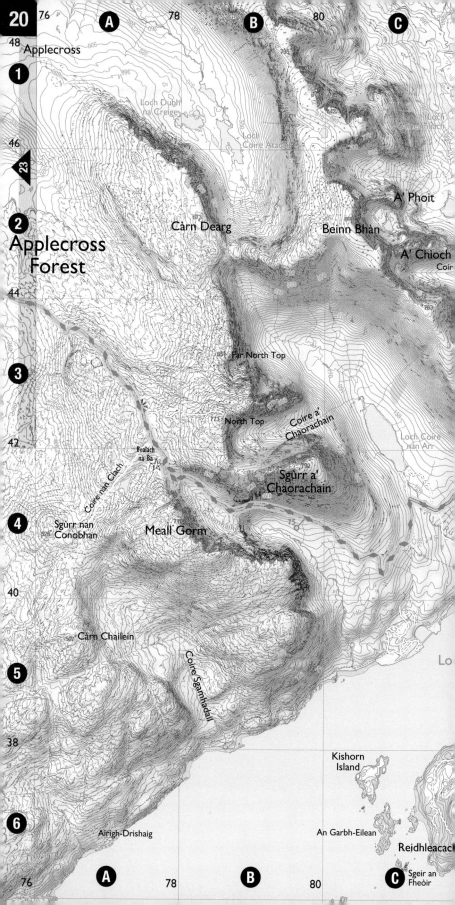

76 | A | 78 | B | 80 | C

48
Applecross

1

46

23

2

Applecross
Forest

Càrn Dearg

Beinn Bhàn

A' Phoit

A' Chioch

Coir

44

3

851 Far North Top

Loch Dubh
na Creige

Loch
Coire Atac

Loch
Gaineamhach

773 North Top

Coire a'
Chaorachain

Loch Coire
nan Arr

42

Bealach
na Bà

Sgùrr a'
Chaorachain

Coire nan Clach

4

Sgùrr nan
Conobhan
826

Meall Gorm

40

Càrn Chailein
507

Coire Sgamhadail

5

38

Kishorn
Island

Lo

6

Airigh-Drishaig

An Garbh-Eilean

Reidhleacac

Sgeir an
Fheòir

76 | A | 78 | B | 80 | C

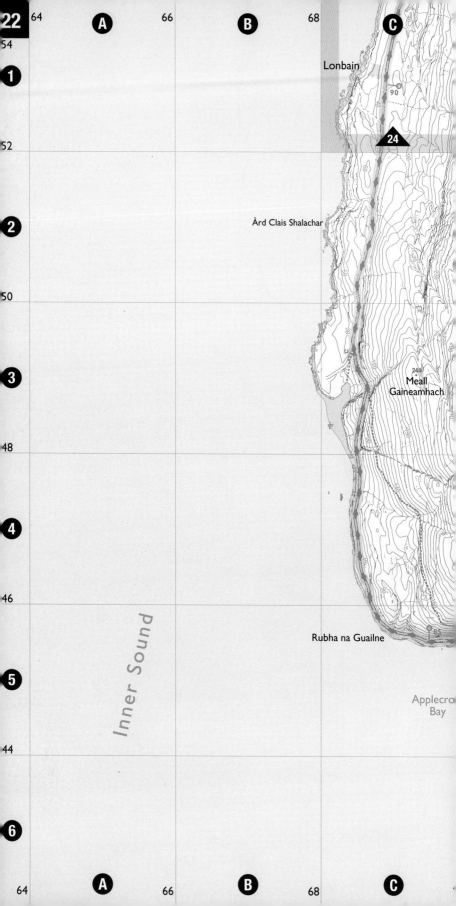

22

Lonbain

Àrd Clais Shalachar

Meall
Gaineamhach

Rubha na Guailne

Inner Sound

Applecro
Bay

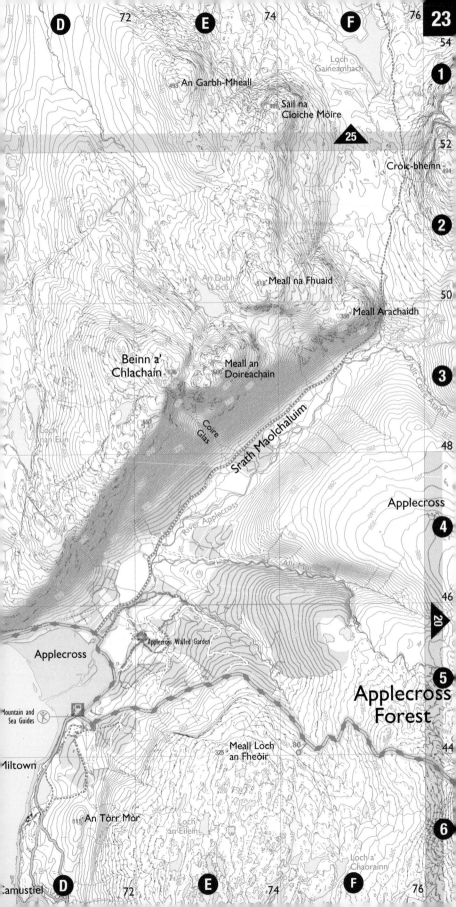

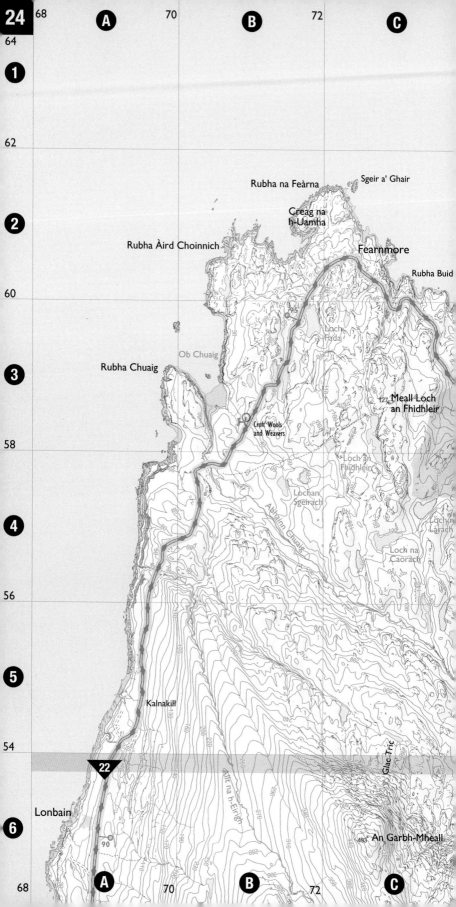

D 76 E 78 F 80

64

1

62

Sithean a' Mhill

2

60

Lower Diabaig

Loch Diabaig

Meall Ceann
na Creige

ha na Mòine

3

Loch Torridon

Meall na
h-Araid

58

Arinacrinachd /
Arrina

Rubha Glas

Eilean Mòr

Sròn a'
Mahàis

Àird

4

Meall na
Coille

Kenmore

Loch a'
Chracaich

Ardheslaig

56

100

A' Bhainlir

Loch
Bhraighaig

Loch Shieldaig

26

Meall an
t-Siomlair

Eilean an
Inbhire Bhàin

Loch a' Choire
Bhuidhe

Sgeirean
Mòra

5

Eilean Dùghaill

Rubha
an Ròin

Meall Dearg

Loch
a' Mhuilinn

54

Loch a'
Chaorainn

23

105

Loch
Ceopach

6

Loch
Gaineamhach

na
che Mòire

D 76 E 78 F 80

An Ruadh-Mheallan

Be
Tom
Gruagai

Loch a
Mhullaich

Upper Diabaig

Meall Ceann
na Creige

Loch
Diabaigas Àirde

Creag an
Fhraoich

Wester Alligin

Inveralligin

Rubha
a' Ghiuthais

Eilean a' Chaoil

Upper Loch
Torridon

Bad Callda

Loch Shieldaig

Rubha na Feòla

Sgeirean Mòra
Eilean Dùghaill

Shieldaig
Island

Meall a'
Choire Bhuidhe

Àird a'
Mheallaidh

Rubha
an Ròin

Ob Mheallaidh

Sildeag /
Shieldaig

Shieldaig
Camping
and Cabins

A896

Coille
Creag-Loch

Ben Shieldaig

Loch an Eun

529

Coire Doire Aonair

Loch
Dùghaill

An Fùr

387

Glen
Shieldaig

Coire Mhurchaidh

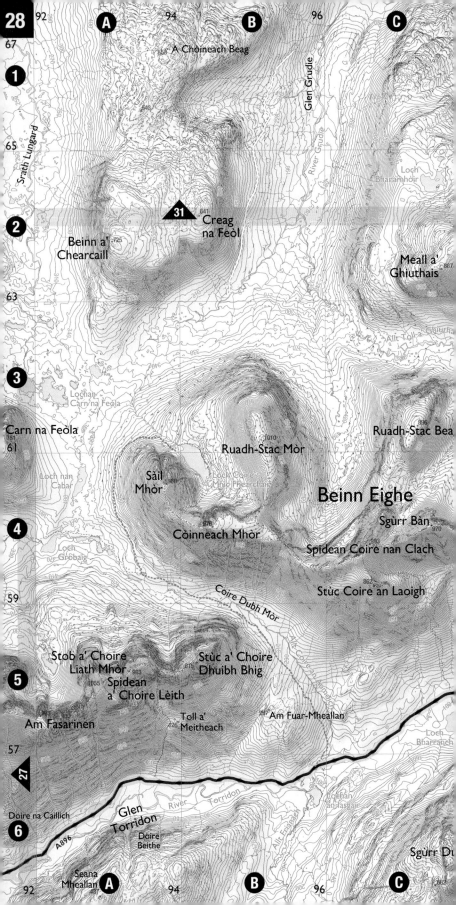

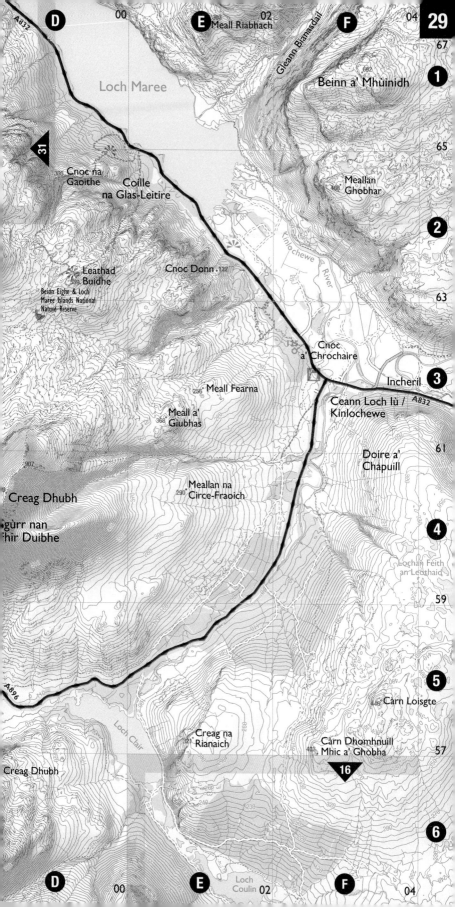

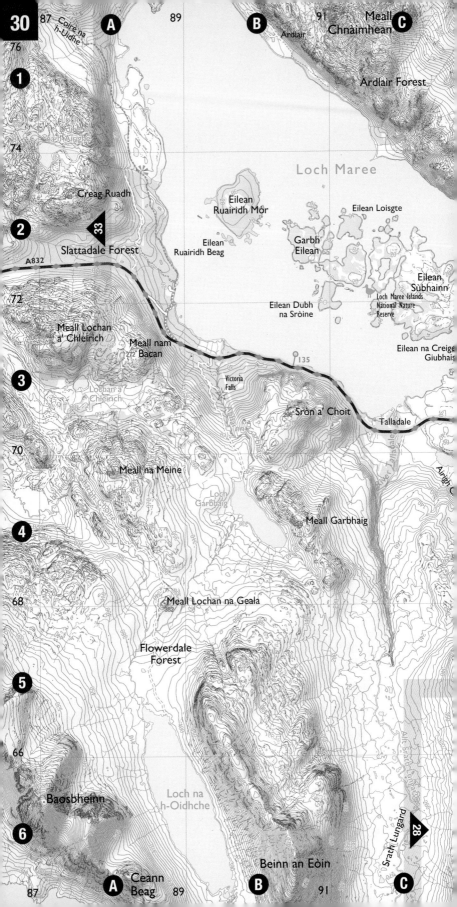

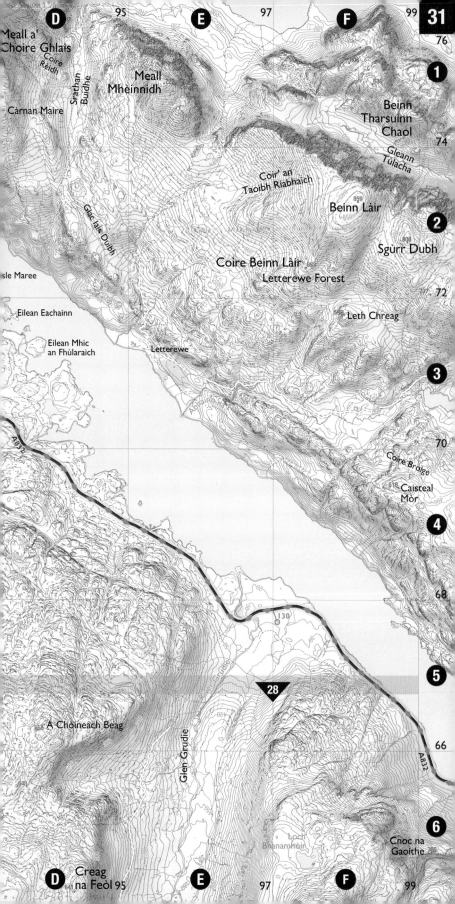

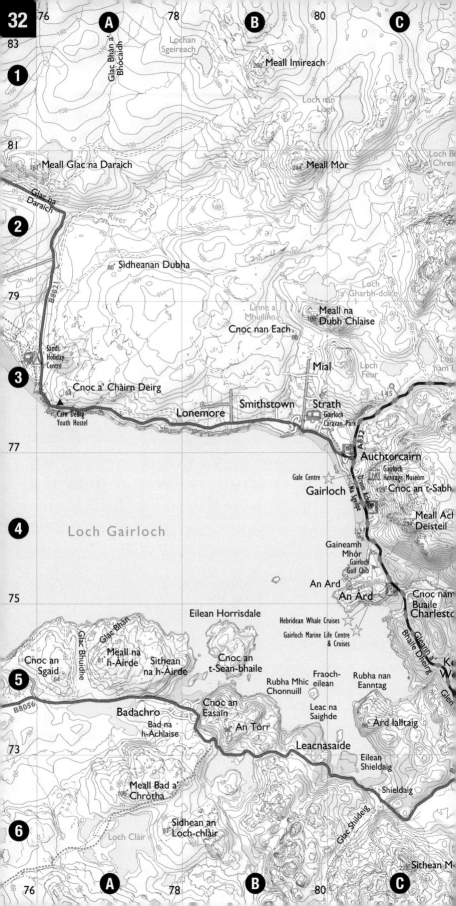

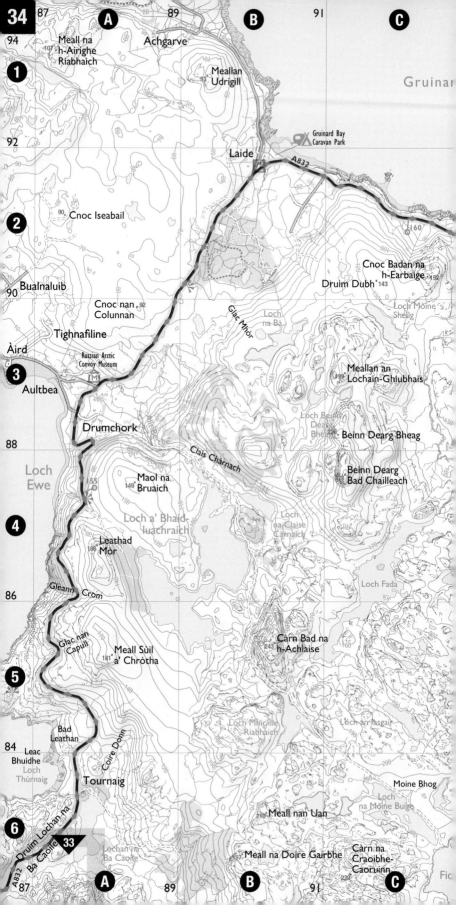

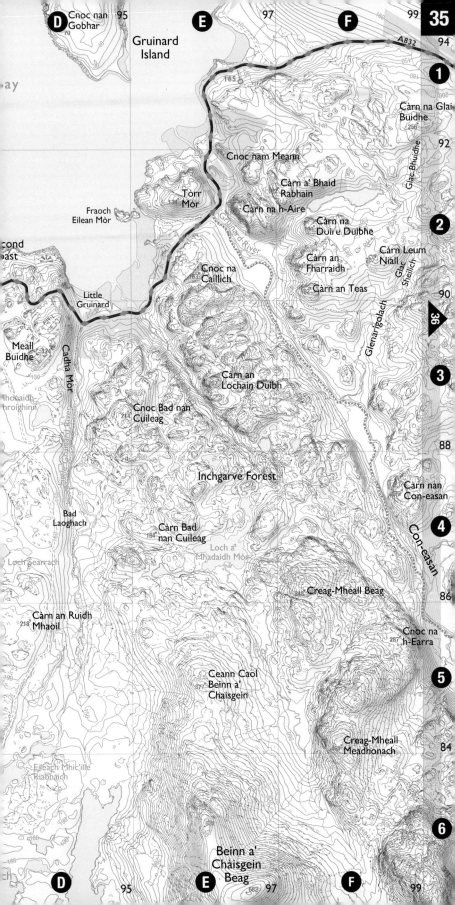

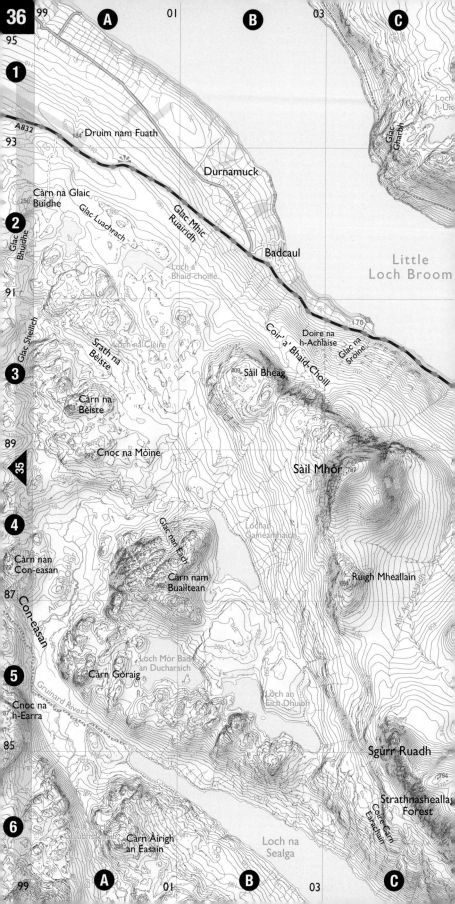

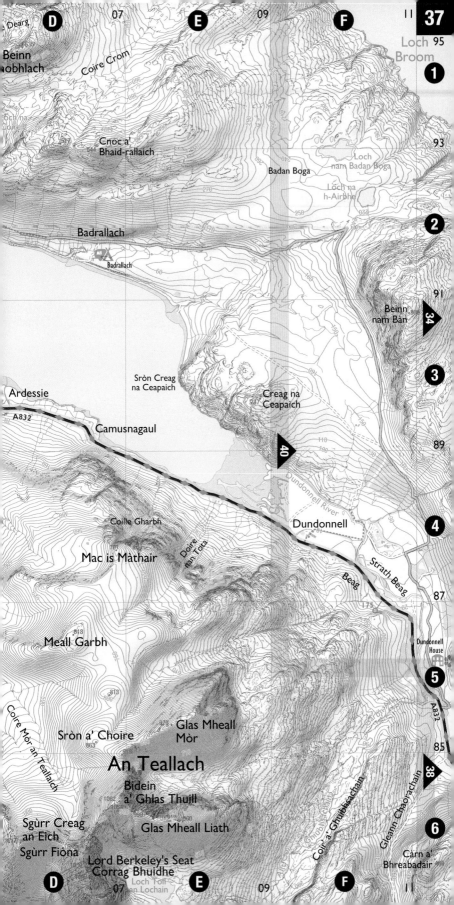

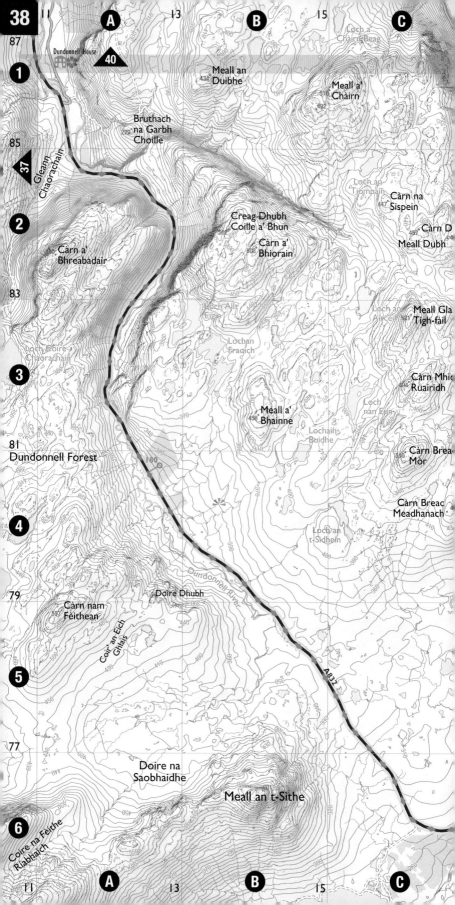

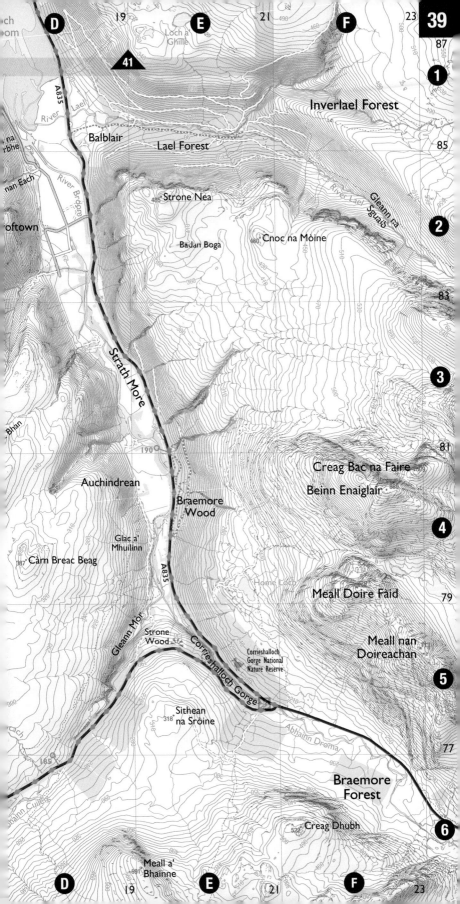

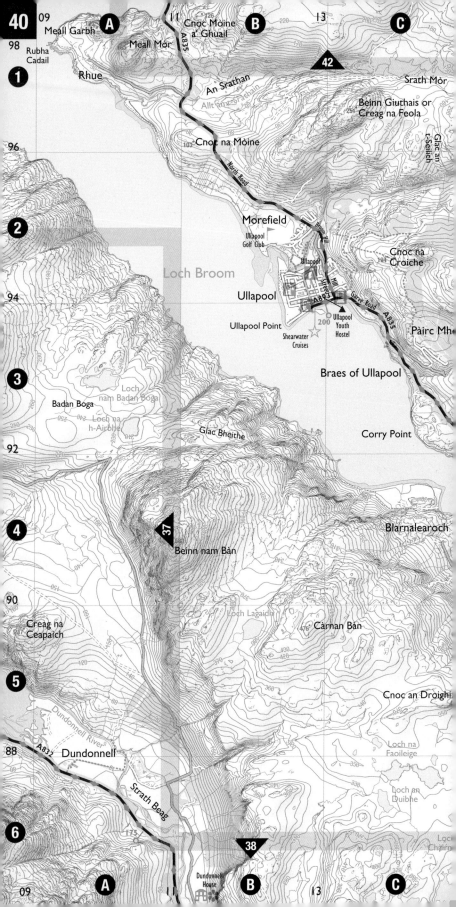

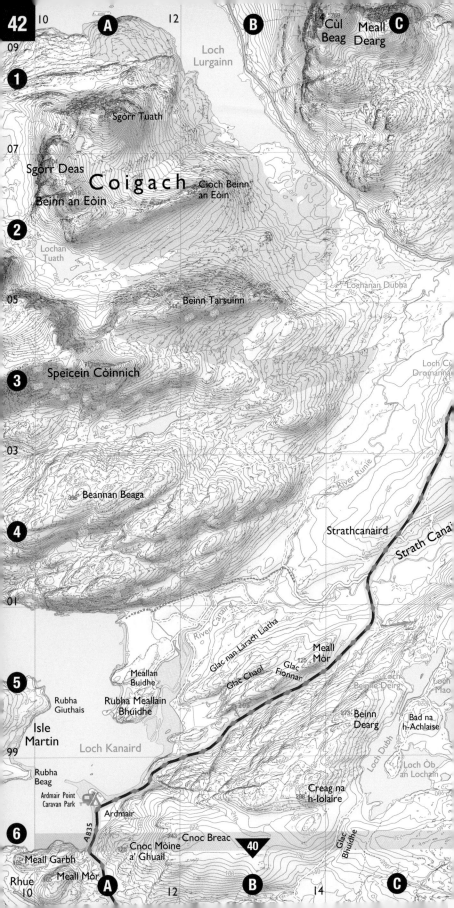

17 A 19 B 21 C

20

1

Loch na
Gainimh

Loch Dubh
Meallan Mhurghaidh
Loch na
Faoileige

Meallan
Mhurchaidh

Meallan
Liath M

Canisp

18

46

Gleann Dorcha

Meall Beag

Glac na Craoibhe
Caorruinn

Meall a'
Mhuthaich

Lochan Fada

2

16 Lochan Rac

Meall na Braclaich

Creag a'
Chroisg

3

Cnoc an
Leathaid Bhig

14

Creagan Mòr

Cam Loch

Loch Veyatie

Cnoc an
Ruadhlaich

Eilean na
Gartaig

Cnoc na
Gaoithe

4

12

Meallan
Diomhain

Ailbhinn /
Elphin

215

Cnoc Breac

5

Cnoc nan Stalcan

174

Knockan

Drumrunie
Forest

10

Lochan
Fhionnlaidh

Glac
Mhaolagain

Cnoc a'
Choilich Beag

Cnoc a'
Choilich Mòr

Knockan Crag
National
Nature Reserve

6

Loch nan Ealachan
Lochan Fada

Cnoc an
Sasannaich

43

Druim
Donn

A

A835

19

Glac Fearna

B

21

C

17

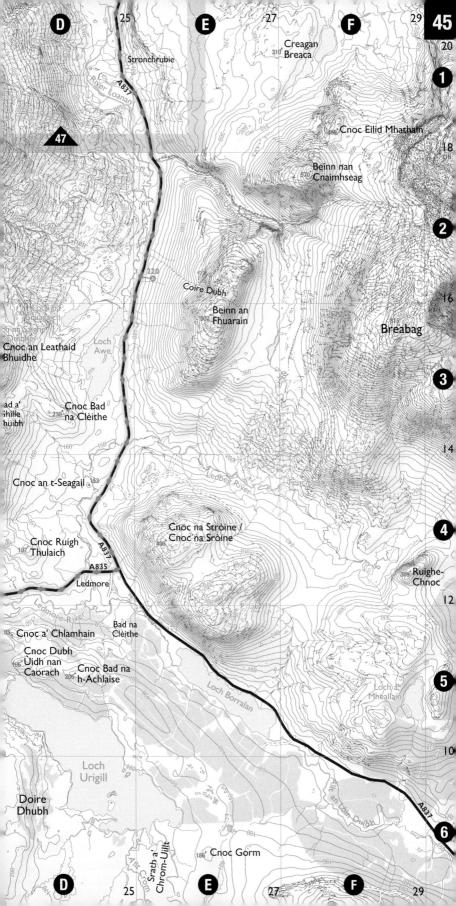

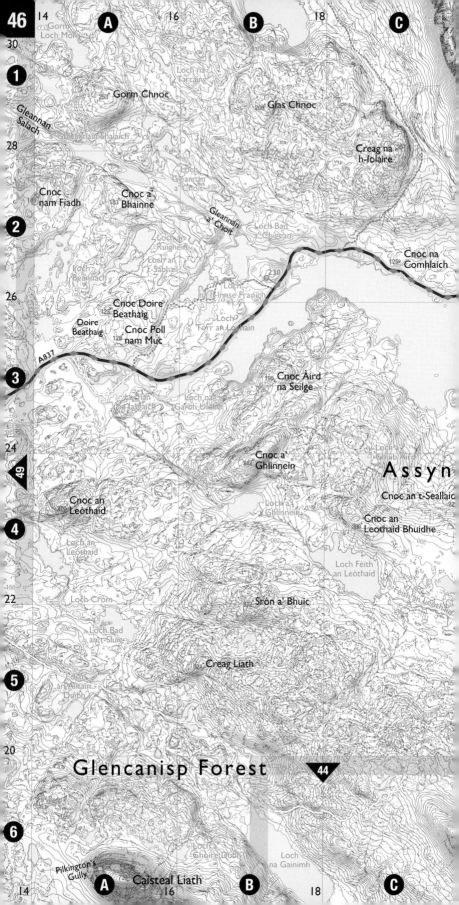

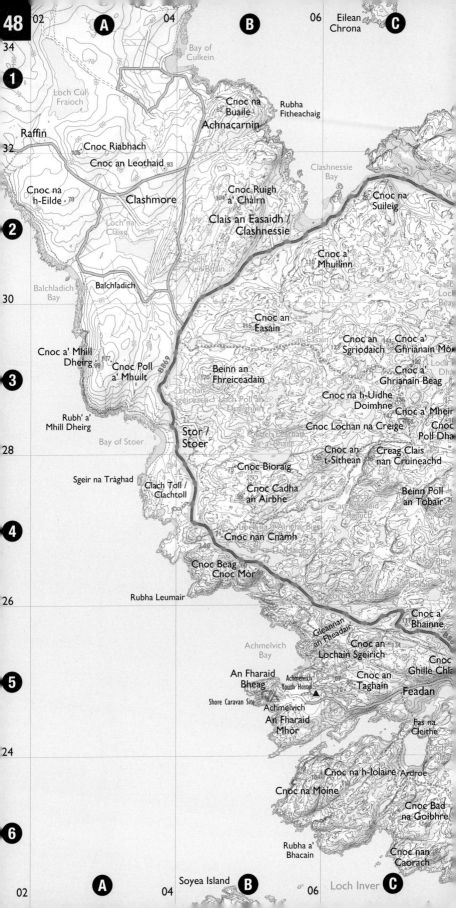

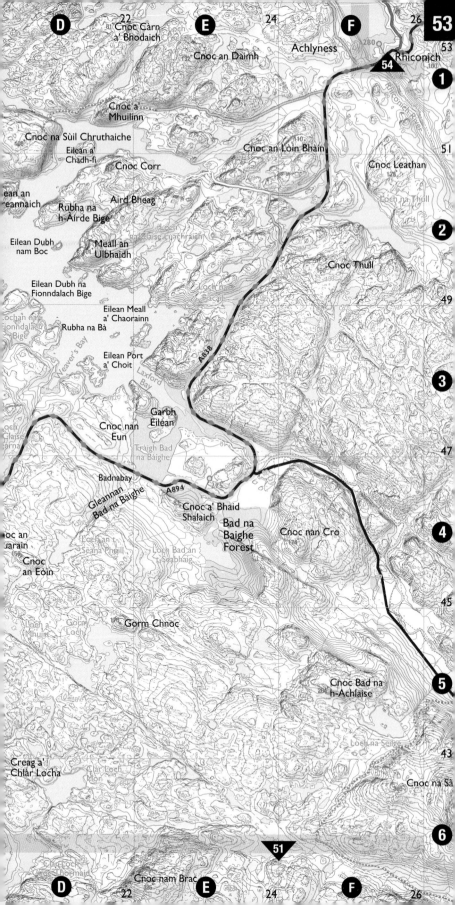

Cnoc an Daimh

Achlyness

Rhiconich

Cnoc a' Mhuilinn

Cnoc na Sùil Chruthaiche

Eilean a' Chadh-fi

Cnoc Corr

Cnoc an Loin Bhàin

Cnoc Leathan

Loch na Thull

ean an reannaich

Aird Bheag

Rubha na h-Àirde Bige

Eilean Dubh nam Boc

Meall an Ulbhaidh

Loch na Claise Lunnraich

Cnoc Thull

Eilean Dubh na Fionndalach Bige

Loch na Piacail

ochan nas ionndalach Bige

Eilean Meall a' Chaorainn

Rubha na Bà

Eilean Port a' Choit

A838

Weaver's Bay

Laxford Bay

Garbh Eilean

Cnoc nan Eun

och Claise arna

Tràigh Bad na Bàighe

Badnabay

Gleannan Bad na Bàighe

A894

Cnoc a' Bhaid Shalaich

Bad na Baighe Forest

Cnoc nan Cro

oc an uarain

Cnoc an Eoin

Lochan t Seana Phuill

Loch Bad an t-Seabhaig

Loch a Mhuillin

Gorm Loch

Gorm Chnoc

Cnoc Bad na h-Achlaise

Loch na Seilge

Creag a' Chlàr Lòcha

Clàr Loch Mòr

Cnoc na Sà

Clàr Loch Thormaid

Cnoc nam Brac

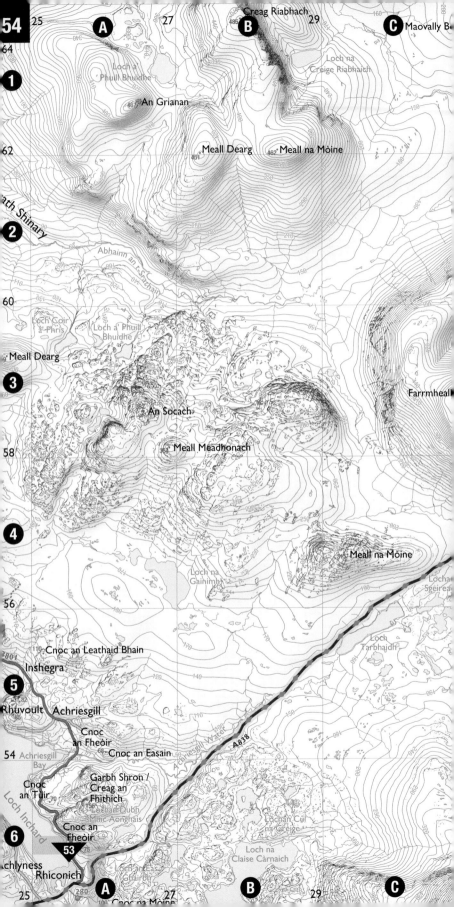

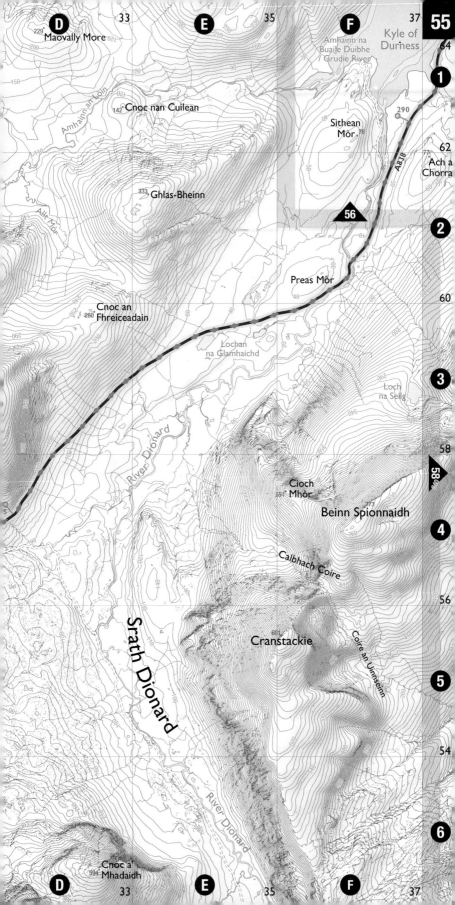

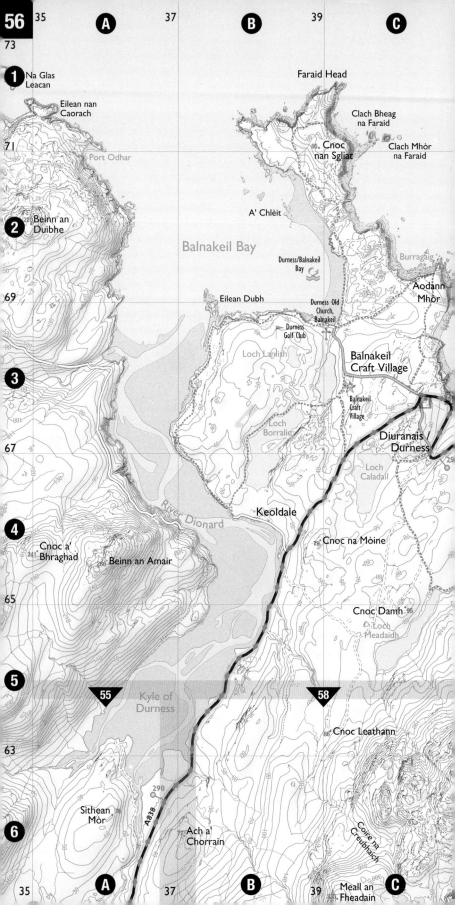

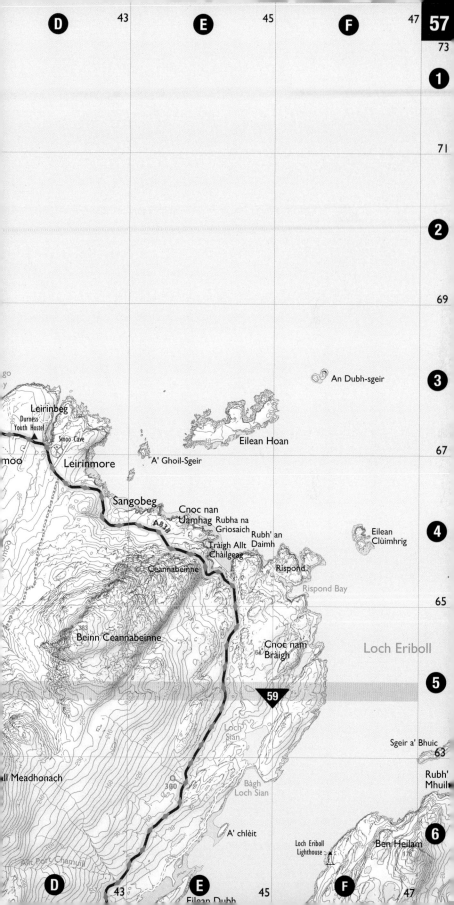

73

1

71

2

69

3

An Dubh-sgeir

go
y

Leirinbeg
Durness
Youth Hostel
Smoo Cave

Eilean Hoan

67

moo Leirinmore

A' Ghoil-Sgeir

Sangobeg

Cnoc nan
Uamhag Rubha na
Griosaich

Eilean
Clùimhrig

4

A838

Rubh' an
Daimh

Tràigh Allt
Chàilgeag

Ceannabeinne

Rispond

Rispond Bay

65

Beinn Ceannabeinne

383

Cnoc nam
Bràigh

Loch Eriboll

5

59

Loch
Sian

Sgeir a' Bhuic

63

ll Meadhonach

Rubh'
Mhuil

Bàgh
Loch Sian

300

A' chlèit

Loch Eriboll
Lighthouse

Ben Heilam

6

Allt Port Chamuill

Eilean Dubh

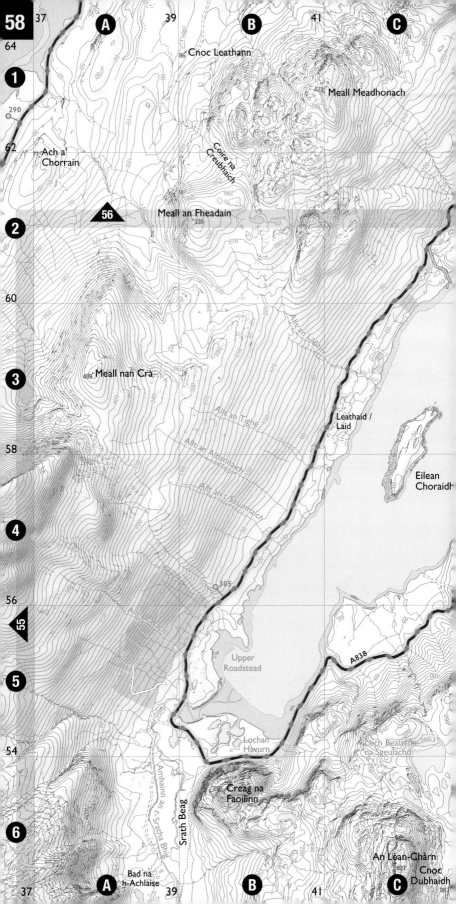

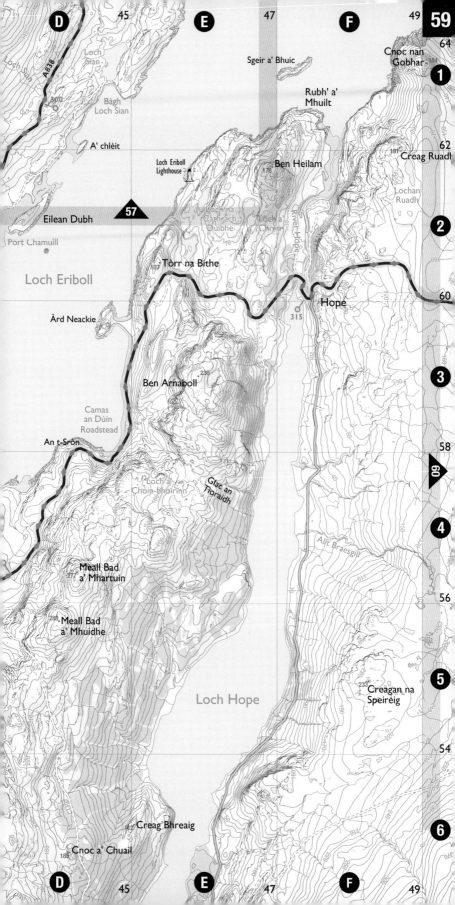

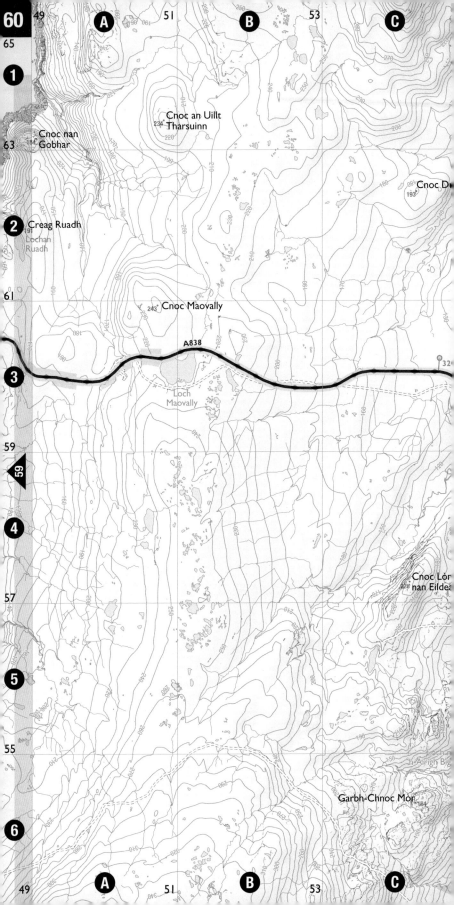

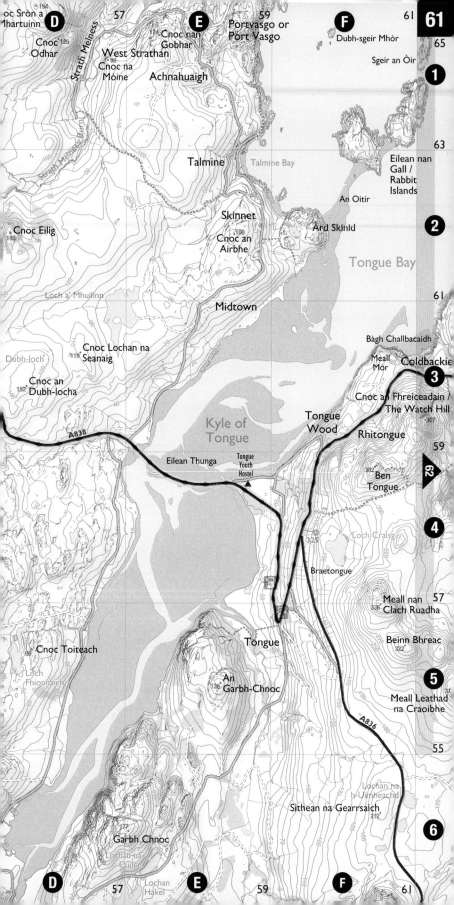

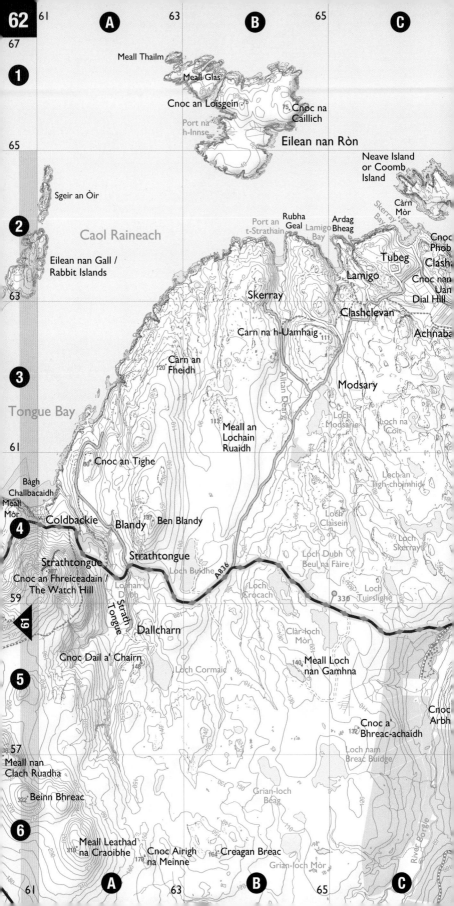

61   **A**   63   **B**   65   **C**

67

1

Meall Thailm

Meall Glas

Cnoc an Loisgein

Cnoc na Caillich

Port na h-Innse

Eilean nan Ròn

65

Neave Island or Coomb Island

Sgeir an Òir

Càrn Mòr

Port an t-Strathain

Rubha Geal

Lamigo Bay

Ardag Bheag

Cnoc Phob

2

Caol Raineach

Tubeg

Clash

Eilean nan Gall / Rabbit Islands

Lamigo

Cnoc nan Uain Dial Hill

Skerray

Clashclevan

Achnaba

63

Carn na h-Uamhaig

Càrn an Fheidh

Modsary

3

Loch Modsarie

Loch na Coit

Tongue Bay

Allt an Dearg

Meall an Lochain Ruaidh

Loch an Tigh-choimhid

61

Cnoc an Tighe

Loch Claisein

Loch Skerray

Bàgh Challbacaidh

Meall Mòr

Coldbackie

Blandy

Ben Blandy

Loch Dubh Beul na Fàire

4

Strathtongue

Strathtongue

Loch Buidhe

A836

Loch Crocach

Loch Tuirslighe

Cnoc an Fhreiceadain / The Watch Hill

Lochan Dubh

330

59

Strath Tongue

Dallcharn

Clàr-loch Mòr

61

Cnoc Dail a' Chairn

Loch Cormaic

Meall Loch nan Gamhna

Cnoc Arbh

5

Cnoc a' Bhreac-achaidh

57

Meall nan Clach Ruadha

Loch nam Breac Buidge

Beinn Bhreac

Grian-loch Beag

6

Meall Leathad na Craoibhe

Cnoc Airigh na Meinne

Creagan Breac

River Borgie

Grian-loch Mòr

61   **A**   63   **B**   65   **C**

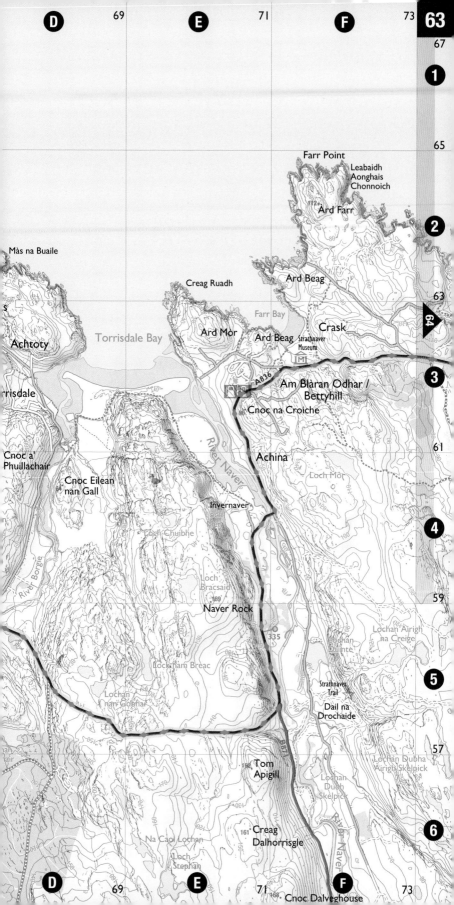

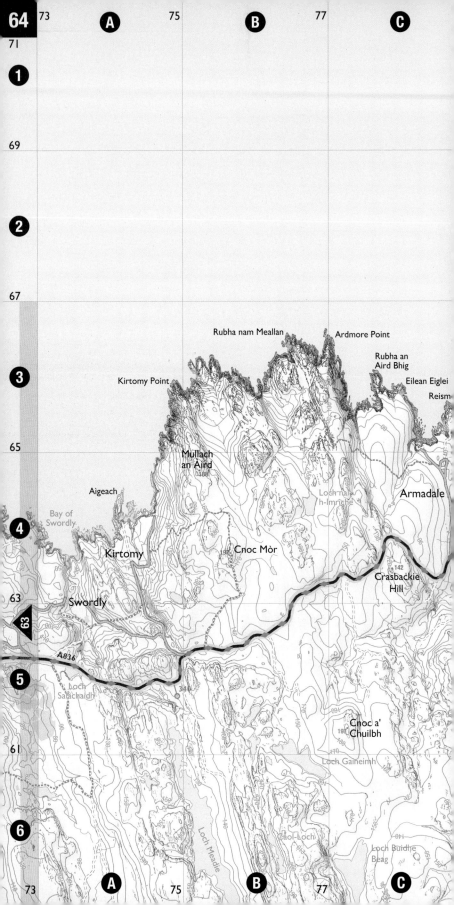

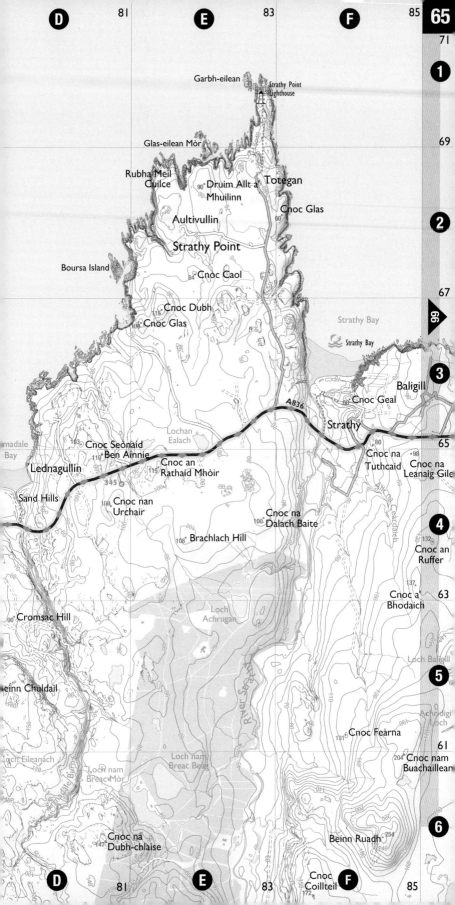

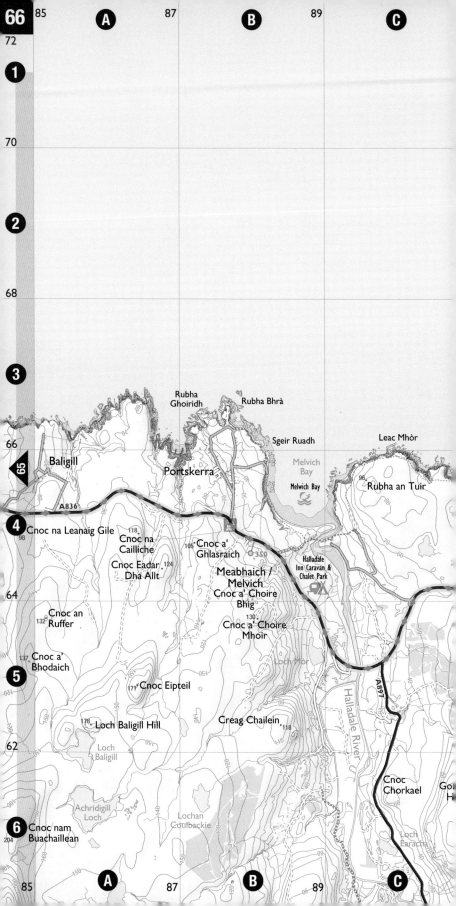

Scarf Rocks

Red Point

Fresgoe

Cnoc Glas

Loch na Moine

Sandside Bay

Cnoc na Moine

102

Reay Golf Club

Reay

A836

355

Cnoc Dachow

Gleann Creagach

Beinn Ruadh

Sandside Burn

Caol-Loch

Beinn Ràtha Bheag

Cnoc an Achadh

Cnoc na Tobaireach

Beinn Ràtha

Loch Garbh

Loch Akran

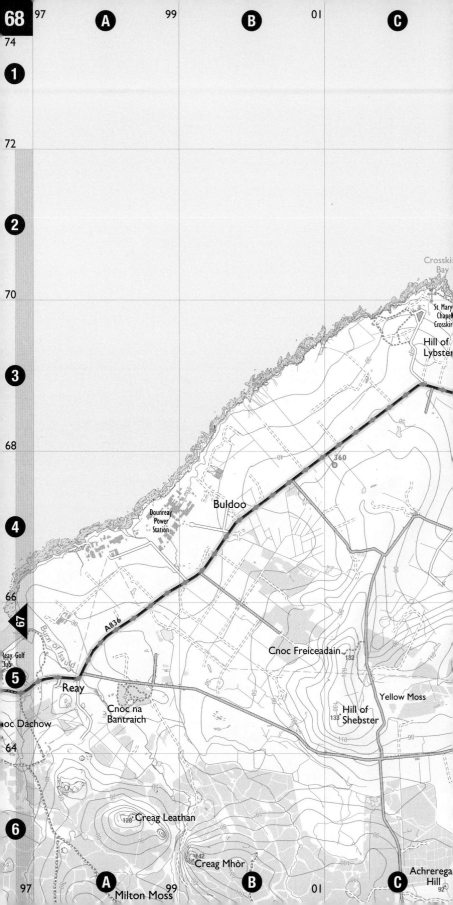

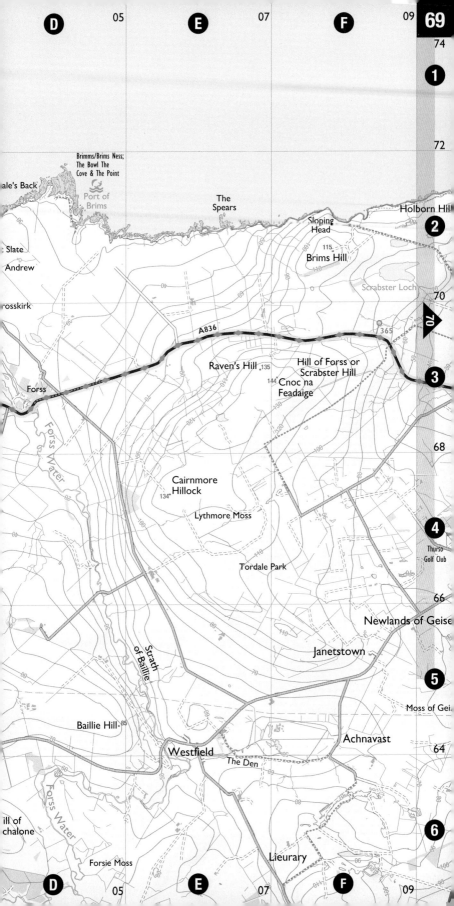

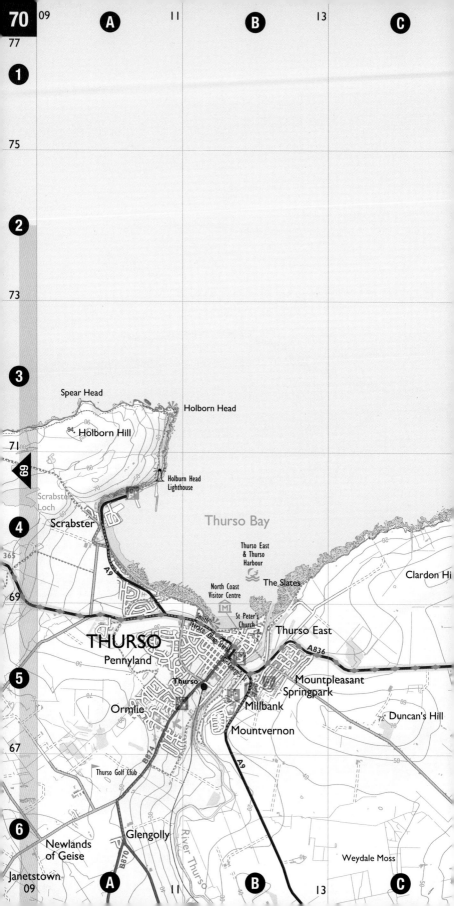

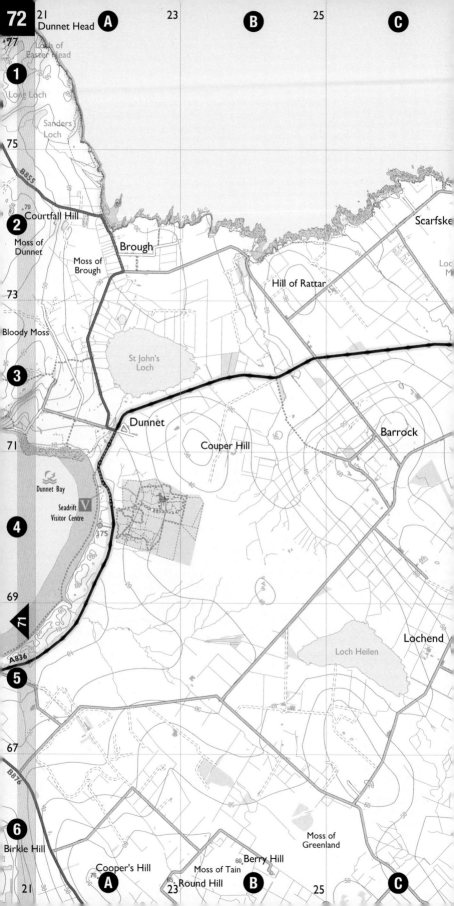

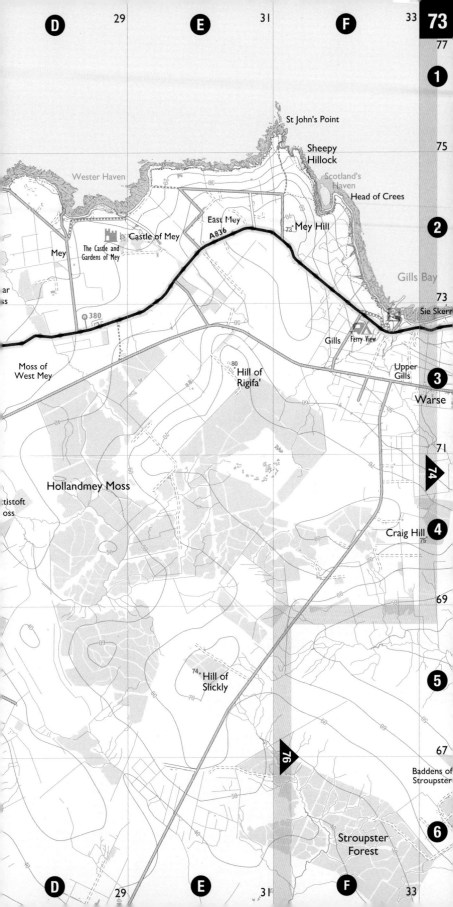

St John's Point

Sheepy
Hillock

Scotland's
Haven

Wester Haven

Head of Crees

East Mey
A836

Mey Hill

Castle of Mey

Gills Bay

Mey

The Castle and
Gardens of Mey

380

Sie Skerr

ar
ss

Gills

Ferry View

Upper
Gills

Moss of
West Mey

Hill of
Rigifa'

80

Warse

Hollandmey Moss

74

tistoft
oss

Craig Hill
75

74 Hill of
Slickly

76

Baddens of
Stroupster

Stroupster
Forest

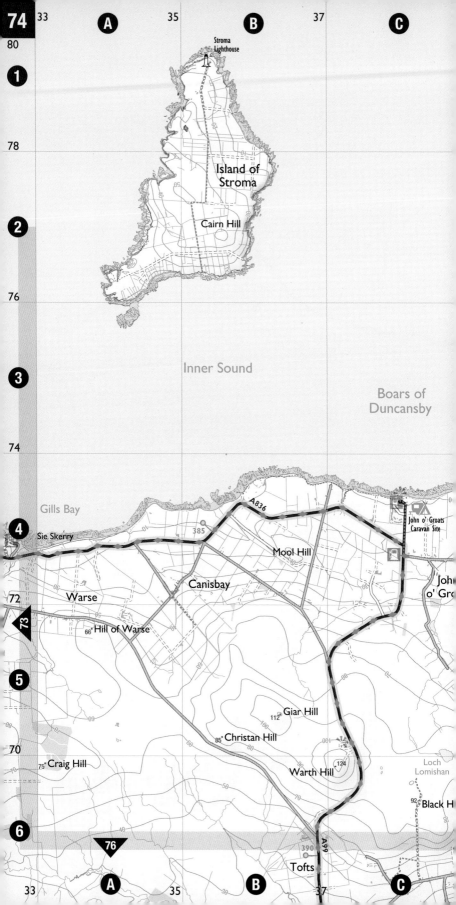

Stroma
Lighthouse

Island of
Stroma

Cairn Hill

Inner Sound

Boars of
Duncansby

Gills Bay

A836

Sie Skerry

385

Mool Hill

Canisbay

John o' Groats
Caravan Site

Joh
o' Gro

Warse

73

66 Hill of Warse

Giar Hill

112

85 Christan Hill

75 Craig Hill

Warth Hill

124

Loch
Lomishan

92 Black H

76

A99

390

Tofts

80

1

78

2

76

3

74

Sannick.

Duncansby Head
Lighthouse

Duncansby
Head   Duncansby Head

4

72

80   Hill of Crogodale

nt Hill
70

5

70

▽ **77**

6

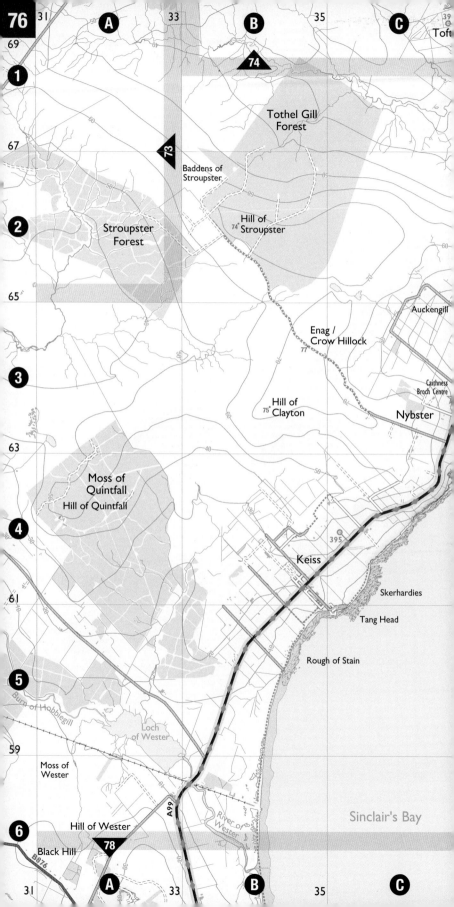

31
A
33
B
35
C
39
Toft

69
1
74
67
73

Tothel Gill
Forest

Baddens of
Stroupster

2
Stroupster
Forest

Hill of
74 Stroupster

65

Auckengill

Enag /
Crow Hillock
77

3
Caithness
Broch Centre

Hill of
75 Clayton

Nybster

63

Moss of
Quintfall

Hill of Quintfall

40

50

4
395

Keiss

61
Skerhardies

Tang Head

Rough of Stain

5
Burn of Hobbiegill

Loch
of Wester

59
Moss of
Wester

A99

River of
Wester

Sinclair's Bay

6
Hill of Wester

78

Black Hill

B876

31
A
33
B
35
C

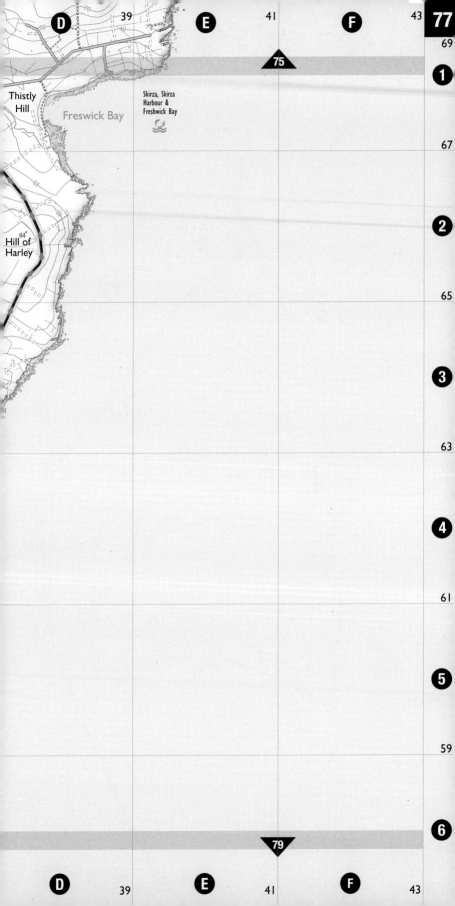

D 39 E 41 F 43 69

▲ 75

1

Thistly
Hill

Freswick Bay

Skirza, Skirza
Harbour &
Freshwick Bay

67

2

65

Hill of
Harley 64'

3

63

4

61

5

59

6

▼ 79

D 39 E 41 F 43

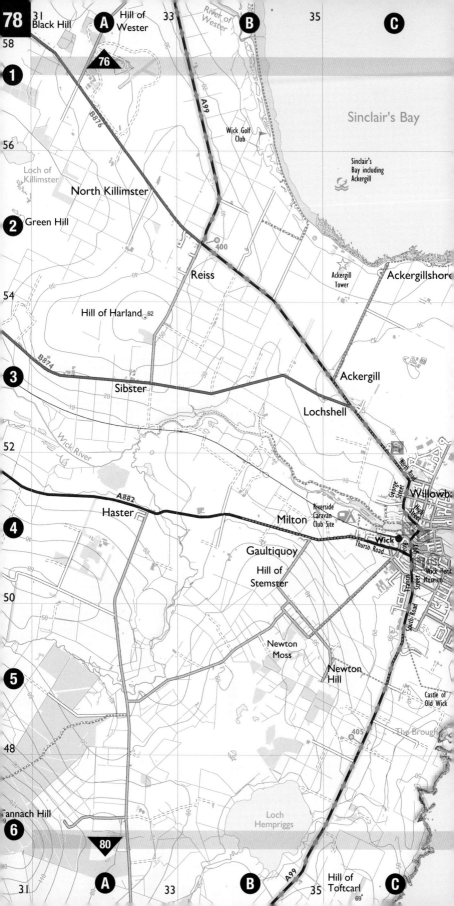

77

Castle Sinclair
Girnigoe

Noss Head

Noss Head
Lighthouse

Staxigoe

Papigoe

Broadhaven

Fas Skerry

Broad
Haven

WICK

Wick Bay

81

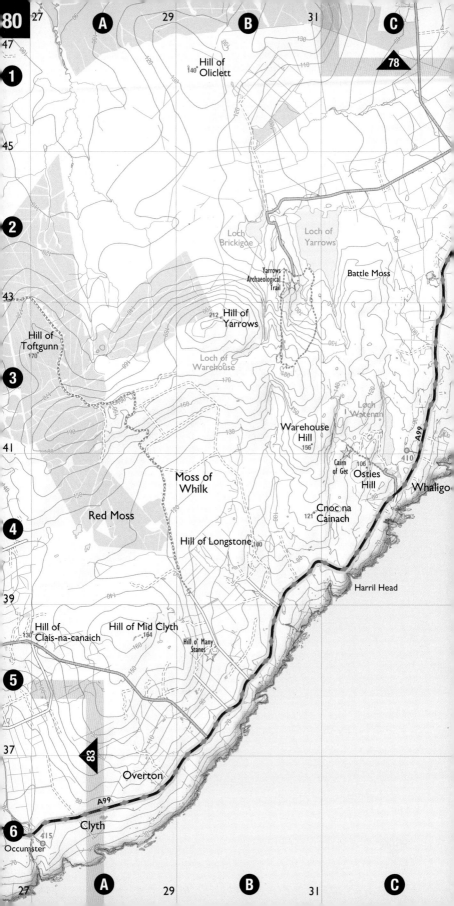

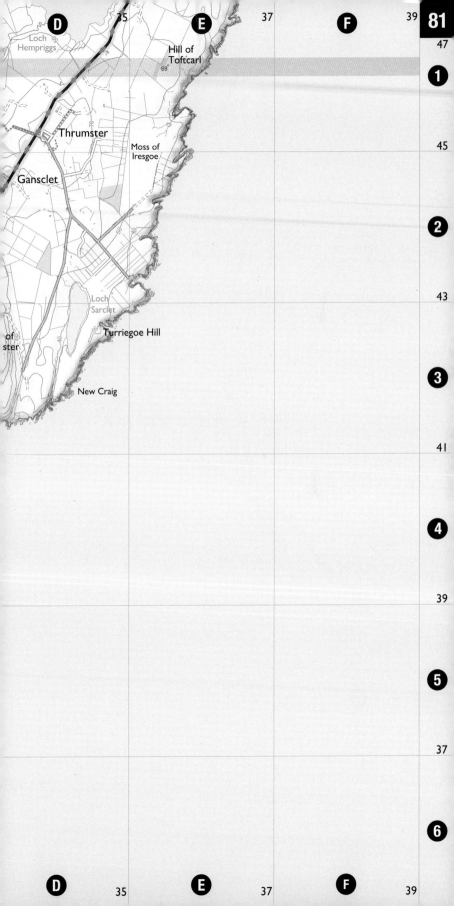

Loch
Hempriggs

Hill of
Toftcarl

Thrumster

Moss of
Iresgoe

Gansclet

Loch
Sarclet

of
ster

Turriegoe Hill

New Craig

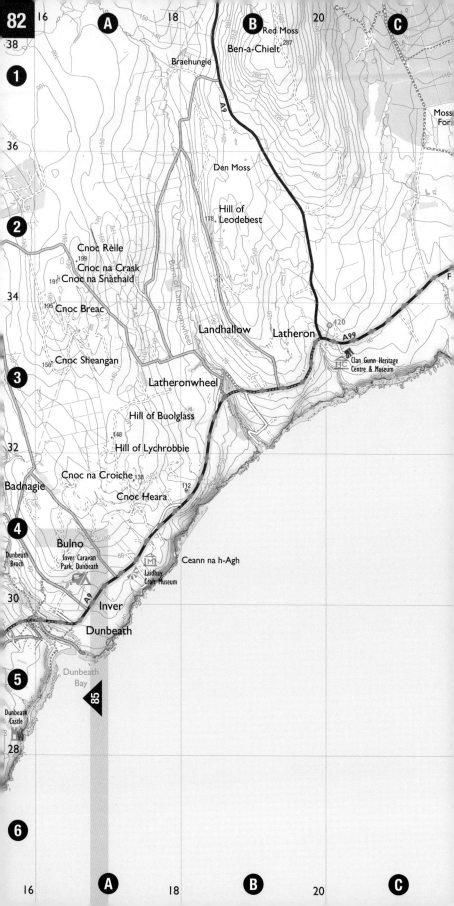

16 **A** 18 **B** 20 **C**

38

1

150

Braehungie

Red Moss

Ben-a-Chielt

260

A9

36

Den Moss

180

2

Hill of
Leodebest

178

Cnoc Rèile

199

Cnoc na Crask

191

Cnoc na Snàthaid

34

195

Cnoc Breac

Burn of Latheronwheel

Landhallow

Latheron

420

A99

F

3

Cnoc Sheangan

150

Latheronwheel

Clan Gunn Heritage
Centre & Museum

Hill of Buolglass

32

148

Hill of Lychrobbie

Cnoc na Croiche

138

Badnagie

112

Cnoc Heara

4

Bulno

Dunbeath
Broch

Inver Caravan
Park, Dunbeath

80

Ceann na h-Agh

Laidhay
Croft Museum

30

A9

Inver

Dunbeath

5

Dunbeath
Bay

85

Dunbeath
Castle

28

6

16 **A** 18 **B** 20 **C**

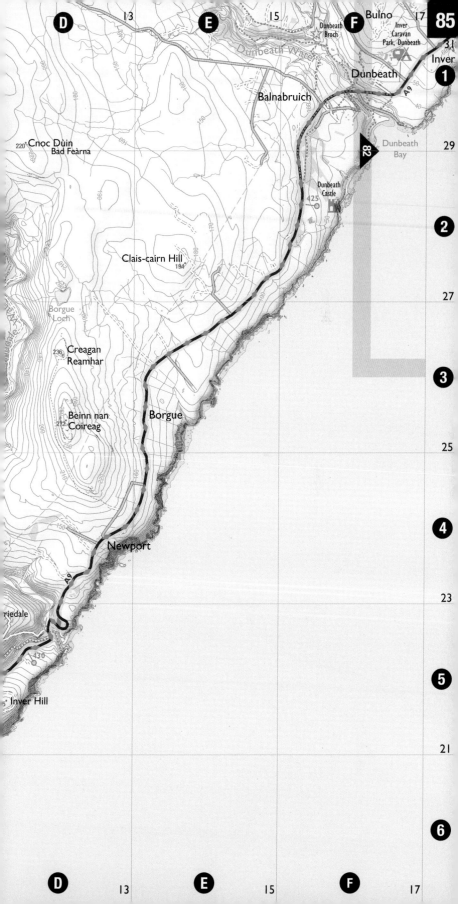

Dunbeath Broch

Inver Caravan Park, Dunbeath

31

Inver

1

Dunbeath Water

Dunbeath

Balnabruich

A9

40

29

220 Cnoc Dùin
Bad Feàrna

Dunbeath Bay

2

Dunbeath Castle
425

50

Clais-cairn Hill
194

27

Borgue Loch

3

236 Creagan Reamhar

Borgue

25

212 Beinn nan Coireag

4

Newport

A9

23

riedale

430

5

Inver Hill

21

6

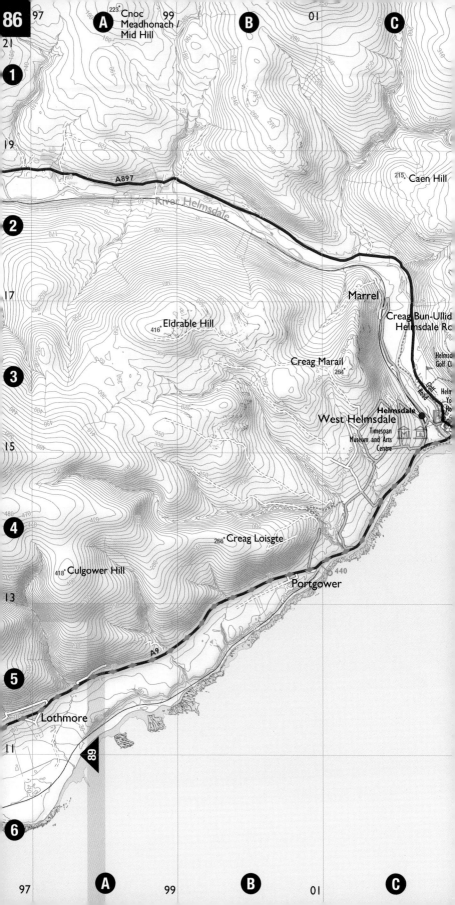

Cnoc Meadhonach / Mid Hill

A897

River Helmsdale

Caen Hill

Marrel

Creag Bun-Ullid
Helmsdale Rc

Eldrable Hill

Creag Marail

Helmsc
Golf Cl

Helm
Yo
Ro

Helmsdale

West Helmsdale

Timespan
Museum and Arts
Centre

Creag Loisgte

Culgower Hill

Portgower

A9

Lothmore

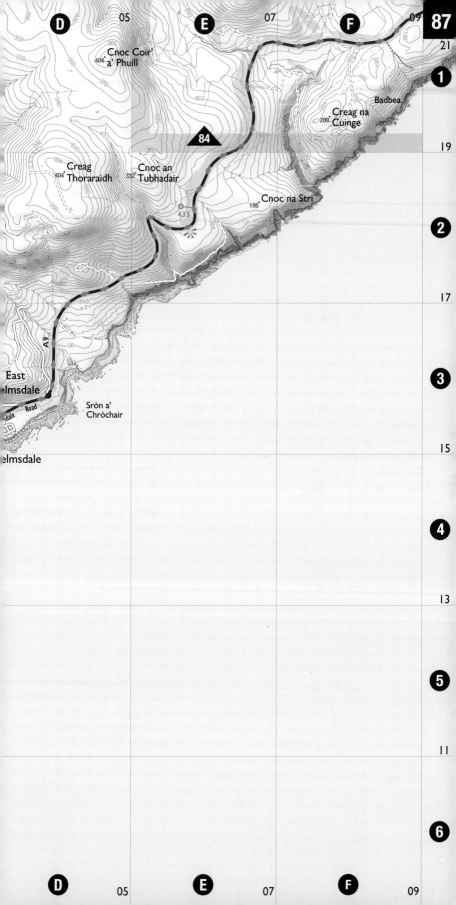

D 94 E 96 Creag Riasgain F 98

Creag Riabhach

Creag a' Chrionaich

Cnoc na h-Iolaire

Glen Loth

Lothmore

A9

Lothbeg

Road

D 94 E 96 F 98

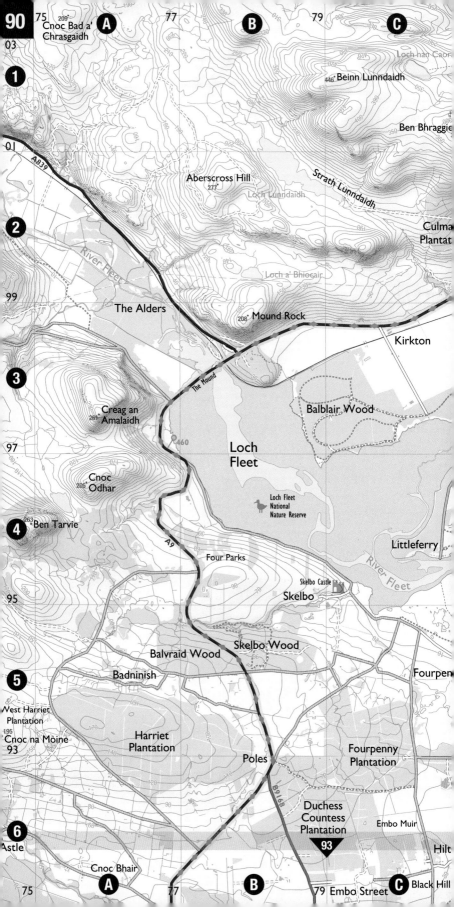

Dunrobin Wood

Ben Bhraggie Wood

Highland
Wildcat
Trails

Dunrobin
Castle

01

Golspie

Dunrobin
Castle

A9

Cnoc na
Croiche

Main Street

Golspie Station Road

Golspie

455

2

99

Golspie Golf Club

3

Ferry
Wood

97

4

95

5

93

Grannie's
Heilan' Hame
Holiday Park

bo

Embo Rocks

6

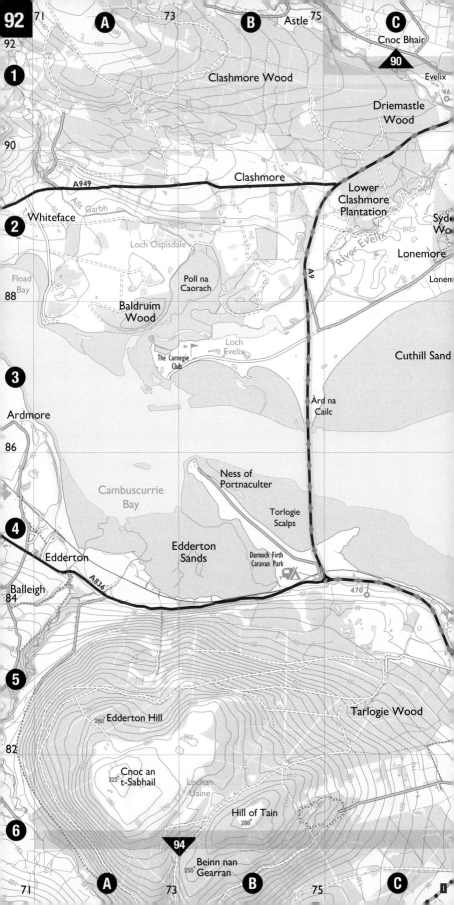

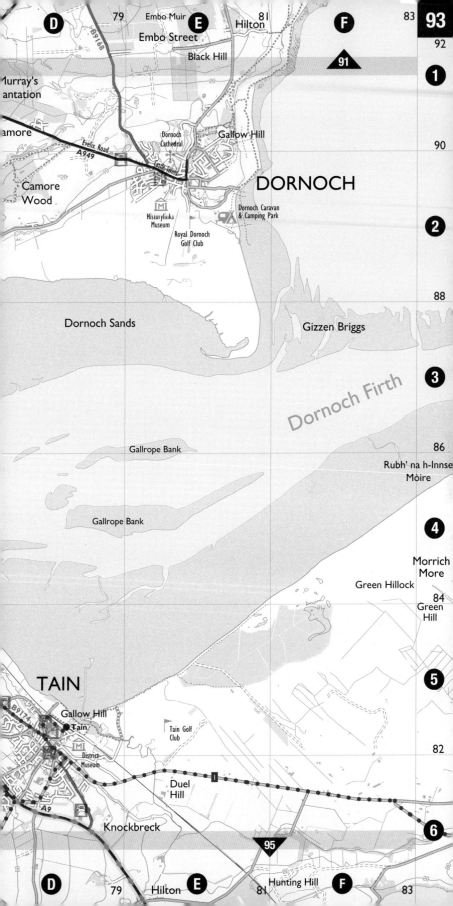

D   79   Embo Muir   **E**   81   Hilton   **F**   83

Embo Street

Black Hill

Murray's
Plantation

91

1

B9168

Dornoch
Cathedral   Gallow Hill

Sycamore

Evelix Road
A949

Earls Street

Camore

DORNOCH

90

Camore
Wood

Historylinks
Museum

Dornoch Caravan
& Camping Park

2

Royal Dornoch
Golf Club

88

Dornoch Sands

Gizzen Briggs

3

Dornoch Firth

Gallrope Bank

86

Rubh' na h-Innse
Mòire

Gallrope Bank

4

Morrich
More

Green Hillock

84
Green
Hill

5

TAIN

82

Gallow Hill

B9174

Tain

Tain Golf
Club

District
Museum

Duel
Hill

1

A9

6

Knockbreck

95

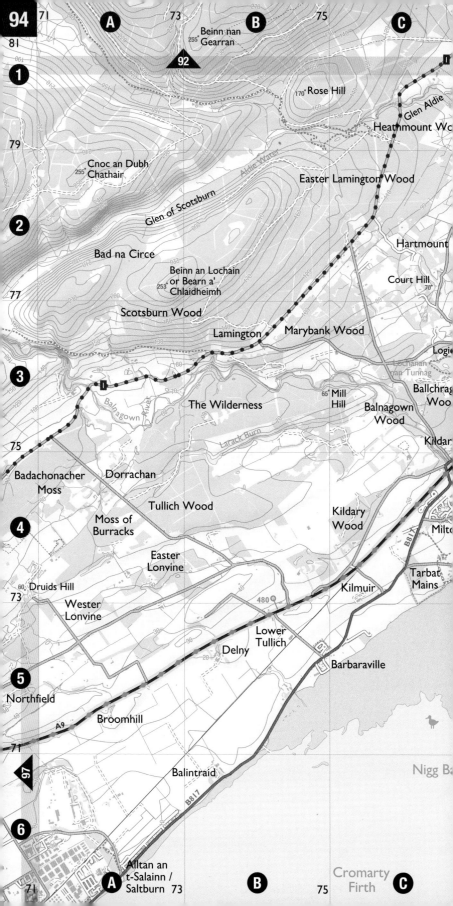

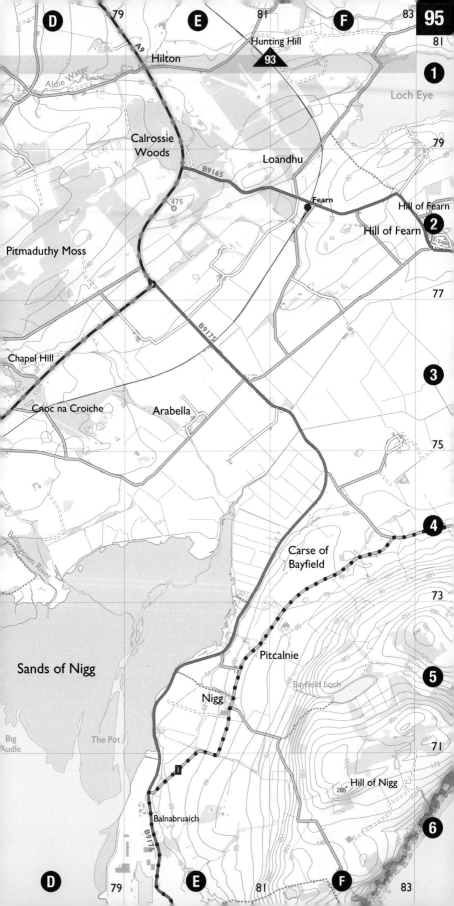

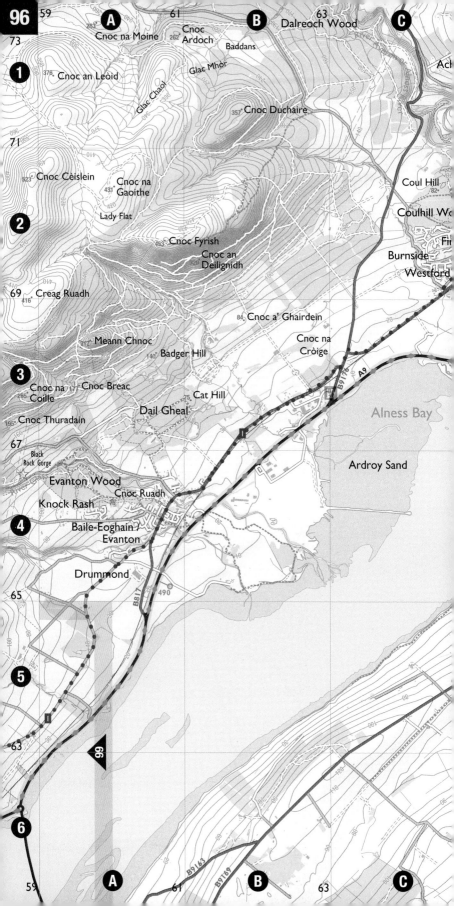

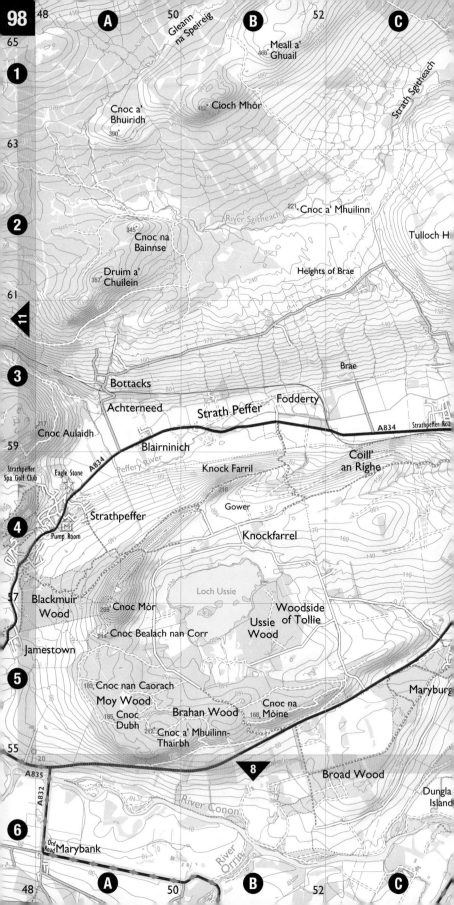

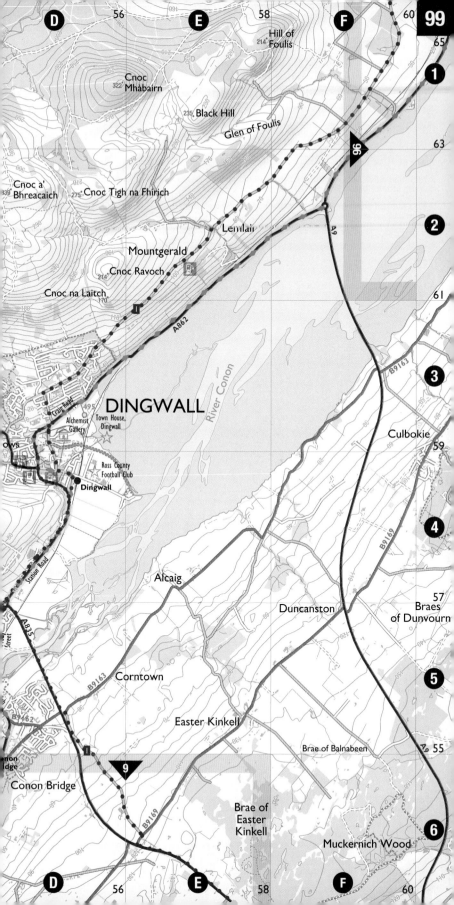

HOW TO USE THIS INDEX

1. The map reference given refers to the actual square in which the feature is located and not the name.

2. A strict alphabetical order is used e.g. Àrd Ialltaig follows Ardheslaig but precedes Ardindrean.

3. Names prefixed with 'The' are indexed under the main name, for example 'The Alders' appears in the A section

THE NATIONAL GRID REFERENCING SYSTEM

The grid lines form part of the National Grid and are at 1 km intervals.

To give a unique reference position of a point to within 100 metres proceed as follows:

Sample point: **Aberscross Hill**

1. Read letters identifying 100,000 metre square in which the point lies (**NC**)

2. FIRST QUOTE EASTINGS - locate the first VERTICAL grid line to the LEFT of the point and read the BLUE figures labelling the line the top or bottom margin of the page (**77**). Estimate tenths from the grid line to the point (**5**). This gives a figure of **775**

3. THEN QUOTE NORTHINGS - locate the first HORIZONTAL grid line BELOW the point and read the BLUE figures labelling the line in the left or right margin of the page (**00**). Estimate tenths from the grid line to the point (**5**). This gives a figure of **005**

Sample reference: **Aberscross Hill NC 775 005**

Aberscross Hill .... 2B 90 NC 775 005	An Àrd .... 4C 32 NG 805 752	Arrina .... 3D 25 NG 744 5
A' Bhainlir .... 4E 25 NC 767 563	An Àrd .... 4C 32 NG 807 751	Asc na Grèine .... 3C 88 NC 900 C
Ach a' Chorrain .... 2A 58 NC 370 619	An Cabar .... 2A 12 NH 257 641	Ashygeo Hillock .... 2E 71 ND 183 7
Achadh na Seileach ... 5A 16 NH 002 481	An Druim Beag .... 1F 49 NC 122 327	Assynt .... 4C 46 NC 199 2
Achanalt .... 4A 12 NH 252 615	An Dubh-sgeir .... 3F 57 NC 456 680	Astle .... 1B 92 NH 745 9
Achanalt Plantation .... 4B 12 NH 262 617	An Dùn .... 4C 84 ND 103 249	Attadale .... 6C 18 NG 931 3
Achandunie .... 1C 96 NH 644 721	An Fharaid Bheag ...... 5B 48 NC 053 248	Attadale .... 6C 18 NG 928 3
Achantraid .... 5D 21 NG 839 388	An Fharaid Mhòr .... 5B 48 NC 054 244	Attadale Forest .... 6F 19 NG 984 3
Achastle .... 2D 83 ND 231 346	An Fùr .... 6A 26 NG 809 507	Auchindrean .... 4E 39 NH 191 8
Achgarve .... 1B 34 NG 892 935	An Garbh-Chnoc .... 5E 61 NC 583 559	Auchmore Wood .... 3A 8 NH 479 5
Achility .... 5E 11 NH 441 568	An Garbh-Eilean .... 6C 20 NG 808 369	Auchtercairn .... 4C 32 NG 802 7
Achina .... 3E 63 NC 707 610	An Garbh-Mheall .... 1E 23 NG 726 529	Aultbea .... 3A 34 NG 878 8
Achinavish Hill .... 1C 84 ND 090 304	An Grianan .... 1A 54 NC 264 627	Aultivullin .... 2E 65 NC 816 6
Achintee .... 5D 19 NG 941 416	An Groban .... 5D 33 NG 838 749	Aultvaich .... 4C 8 NH 510 4
Achintraid .... 5D 21 NG 839 388	An Leacainn .... 6A 6 NH 577 410	
A' Chìoch .... 2C 20 NG 810 446	An Lèan-Chàrn .... 6C 58 NC 419 525	
A' Chlèit .... 2B 56 NC 384 701	An Liathanach .... 4A 14 NH 123 568	Badachonacher .... 1F 97 NH 693 7
A' chlèit .... 6E 57 NC 443 620	Annat .... 4E 27 NG 889 541	Badachonacher Moss .. 4A 94 NH 710 7
Achlyness .... 1F 53 NC 248 525	An Nead .... 2F 49 NC 136 319	Bad a' Chreamha ...... 2A 12 NH 243 6
Achmelvich Youth Hostel	An Oitir .... 2F 61 NC 598 621	Bad a' Chreamha ...... 6E 21 NG 857 3
.... 5B 48 NC 059 248	An Ruadh-Mheallan .... 1B 26 NG 836 614	Badachro .... 5A 32 NG 774 7
Achnabat .... 3C 62 NC 662 626	An Ruadh-Stac .... 1C 18 NG 921 480	Bad a' Ghille Dhuibh ... 3D 45 NC 232 1
Achnacarnin .... 2B 48 NC 041 318	An Sgonnan .... 4A 50 NC 158 342	Bad a' Ghrianain .... 5D 49 NC 096 2
Achnagarron .... 2E 97 NH 683 702	An Sgùrr .... 5E 21 NG 856 387	Bad an Achaidh .... 4B 84 ND 086 2
Achnahuaigh .... 1E 61 NC 581 641	An Socach .... 3A 54 NC 265 586	Bad an Aon Tighe ...... 1E 49 NC 113 3
Achnasheen Plantation	An Srathan .... 1B 40 NH 114 967	Badan Boga .... 2F 37 NH 095 9
.... 3C 14 NH 171 595	An t-Sròn .... 3D 59 NC 442 580	Badan Boga .... 2E 39 NH 202 8
Achnashellach .... 5A 16 NH 002 481	An Teallach .... 5D 37 NH 065 852	Badan Ghruidich .... 3D 13 NH 301 6
Achnashellach Forest .. 5B 16 NH 028 480	An Tòrr .... 5B 32 NG 786 733	Bad an Leth Leòid ..... 3F 49 NC 129 2
Achnasoul Wood .... 2B 8 NH 482 519	An Tòrr Mòr .... 6D 23 NG 712 431	Badan Mòr .... 6D 27 NG 873 5
Achnavast .... 5F 69 ND 079 643	Aodann Mhòr .... 2C 56 NC 405 692	Badavanich .... 2F 41 NH 190 9
A Chòineach Beag ..... 5D 31 NG 938 663	Aonach Dubh .... 3A 14 NH 136 597	Badbea .... 6B 84 ND 085 1
Achreregan Hill .... 6C 68 ND 026 622	Aonach Dubh .... 3C 16 NH 052 518	Badcall Bay .... 1B 50 NC 160 4
Achriesgill .... 5A 54 NC 255 540	Aonach Pàirc Dhùghaill	Bad Callda .... 4A 26 NG 815 5
Achrimsdale .... 4C 88 NC 906 064	.... 6D 21 NG 829 367	Badcaul .... 2B 36 NH 019 9
Achterneed .... 3A 98 NH 489 595	A' Phoit .... 2C 20 NG 809 453	Baddans of Stroupster
Achtoty .... 3D 63 NC 676 622	Applecross .... 1A 20 NG 762 473	.... 2B 76 ND 331 6
Ackergill .... 3C 78 ND 351 529	Applecross .... 5D 23 NG 719 453	Baddidarach .... 6D 49 NC 086 2
Ackergillshore .... 2C 78 ND 358 544	Applecross Bay .... 5D 23 NG 706 449	Badenahauglish .... 2C 88 NC 909 0
Ackergill Tower .... 2C 78 ND 352 545	Applecross Forest ..... 2A 20 NG 761 447	Bad Feàrna .... 1D 85 ND 121 2
Adventure Activity Centre	Applecross Walled Garden	Badger Hill .... 3A 96 NH 606 6
.... 4E 27 NG 888 542	.... 5E 23 NG 720 455	Bad Laoghach .... 4D 35 NG 941 8
A' Ghoil-Sgeir .... 3E 57 NC 432 670	Arabella .... 3E 95 NH 799 753	Bad Leathan .... 5A 34 NG 875 8
Aìgeach .... 4A 64 NC 740 642	Arcan Muir .... 2B 8 NH 487 529	Bad na Baighe Forest .. 4E 53 NC 234 4
Àird .... 4F 25 NG 783 571	Ardachew .... 5B 88 NC 895 043	Bad na Cìrce .... 2A 94 NH 721 7
Àird a' Mheallaidh ...... 4B 26 NG 834 544	Ardag Bheag .... 2C 62 NC 651 637	Bad na Clèithe .... 5D 45 NC 248 1
Aird an Iall .... 1E 49 NC 117 324	Ardarroch .... 5D 21 NG 836 397	Bad na h-Achlaise ..... 5A 32 NG 777 7
Aird an t-Sabhail .... 1E 49 NC 118 327	Ard Beag .... 2F 63 NC 712 632	Bad na h-Achlaise ..... 5C 42 NH 153 9
Aird Bheag .... 2D 53 NC 216 503	Ardcharnich .... 5E 41 NH 173 886	Bad na h-Achlaise ..... 6A 58 NC 385 5
Àird da Loch .... 5F 51 NC 251 325	Àrd Clais Shalachar .... 2C 22 NG 681 510	Badnambreac .... 2E 49 NC 108 3
Àird Mhòr .... 4D 27 NG 860 550	Ardessie .... 3D 37 NH 052 896	Bad nan Aighean ...... 5F 49 NC 134 2
Alcaig .... 4E 99 NH 566 572	Àrd Farr .... 2F 63 NC 716 642	Bad nan Carbad .... 3E 47 NC 223 2
Alchemist Gallery ...... 3D 99 NH 551 592	Ardheslaig .... 4F 25 NG 782 567	Badnellan .... 5B 88 NC 886 C
Alders, The .... 2A 90 NH 762 990	Àrd Ialltaig .... 5C 32 NG 805 734	Badninish .... 5A 90 NH 767 S
Allanglach Wood .... 1D 7 NH 632 505	Ardindrean .... 6D 41 NH 159 879	Badrallach .... 2D 37 NH 062 9
Alltan an t-Salainn ..... 6A 94 NH 722 695	Ardlair Forest .... 1C 30 NG 920 749	Bàgh Challbacaidh ..... 3F 61 NC 609 6
Alltan Dubh / Black Water	Ardmair Point Caravan Park	Baile-Eoghain .... 4A 96 NH 606 6
.... 2B 10 NH 394 625	.... 6A 42 NH 107 984	Baillie Hill .... 5D 69 ND 049 6
Alltan Dubh / Black Water	Àrd Mòr .... 3E 63 NC 700 625	Balblair .... 1D 39 NH 181 8
.... 5E 11 NH 448 576	Ardmore Point .... 1C 52 NC 183 515	Balblair .... 4F 97 NH 706 6
Alness .... 2D 97 NH 660 695	Ardmore Point .... 3B 64 NC 769 662	Balblair Wood .... 3C 90 NH 791 S
Alness Bay .... 3C 96 NH 639 670	Àrd na Cailc .... 3B 92 NH 748 867	Balchladich .... 3C 8 NH 536 4
Alnessferry .... 4D 97 NH 664 660	Ardnagrask .... 3C 8 NH 517 495	Balchraggan Wood ..... 3A 94 NH 725 8
Alness Golf Club .... 2D 97 NH 652 704	Àrd Neackie .... 3D 59 NC 446 597	Balchladich .... 4A 66 NC 853 6
Alness Heritage Centre	Ardroy Sand .... 4C 96 NH 635 669	Baligill .... 6B 94 NH 734 7
.... 3C 96 NH 647 686	Àrd Skinid .... 2F 61 NC 595 620	Ballchraggan Wood .... 3G 94 NH 769 7
Am Beannan .... 4F 21 NG 868 413	Ardvreck Castle .... 4E 47 NC 239 235	Ballifeary .... 4F 7 NH 660 4
Am Blàran Odhar ...... 3E 63 NC 706 620	Arinacrinachd .... 3D 25 NG 744 583	Balnabruich .... 1F 85 ND 157 2
Am Fasarinen .... 5A 28 NG 923 574	Armadale .... 4C 64 NC 786 646	Balnacra .... 2E 19 NG 978 4
Am Fuar-Mheallan ..... 5B 28 NG 952 575	Arpafeelie .... 1C 6 NH 613 504	Balnabruich ....

nagown Wood.........	3C 94	NH 761 755
nakeil Bay............	2B 56	NC 374 699
nakeil Craft Village..	3C 56	NC 393 680
vaird................	2D 9	NH 536 517
vaird Wood...........	2D 9	NH 537 527
vraid Wood...........	5B 90	NH 770 943
osbheinn.............	6A 30	NG 870 654
rbaraville...........	5B 94	NH 749 722
rrock................	3C 72	ND 256 712
ttle Moss...........	2C 80	NH 316 434
alach a' Ghlas-Chnoic		
....	3A 18	NG 890 450
alach na Ba..........	3A 20	NH 776 423
annan Beaga..........	4A 42	NC 105 024
auly................	5D 9	NH 526 463
auly Firth...........	3B 6	NH 584 474
auly Priory..........	5D 9	NH 527 464
inn a' Bhric.........	2F 13	NH 344 651
inn a' Chàisteinn Beag		
....	6E 35	NG 965 821
inn a' Chàit.........	1D 21	NC 027 475
inn a' Chearcaill....	2A 28	NG 930 637
inn a' Chlachain.....	3E 23	NG 724 490
inn a' Ghuilbein....	2D 11	NH 421 635
inn Alligin..........	1D 27	NG 860 605
inn a' Mhùinidh.....	1F 29	NH 032 660
inn an Amair.........	4A 56	NC 360 655
inn an Eòin.........	6B 30	NG 905 646
inn an Eòin.........	2A 42	NC 104 064
inn an Fhreiceadain .	3B 48	NC 044 290
inn an Fhuarain.....	3E 45	NC 260 158
inn an Lochain or Bearn		
a' Chlaidheimh....	2A 94	NH 727 772
inn an t-Sratha.....	4F 41	NH 198 909
inn Bhàn............	2C 20	NG 803 450
inn Bheag...........	5D 27	NG 865 537
inn Bhreac..........	5F 61	NC 608 564
inn Ceannabeinne....	5D 57	NC 422 646
inn Chroisg.........	5F 43	NC 201 009
inn Chuldail........	5D 65	NC 791 618
inn Damh............	6E 27	NG 892 501
inn Dearg...........	1E 27	NG 895 608
inn Dearg...........	5C 42	NH 143 995
inn Dearg Bad Chailleach		
....	4C 34	NG 912 876
inn Dearg Bheag.....	3C 34	NG 911 882
inn Dòmhnaill.......	6E 43	NH 190 981
inn Eighe...........	4C 28	NG 965 605
inn Eighe & Loch Maree		
Islands National		
Nature Reserve...	3D 29	NG 987 627
inn Eilideach.......	3E 41	NH 170 926
inn Enaiglair.......	4F 39	NH 224 805
inn Gharbh..........	4D 47	NC 216 222
inn Ghobhlach.......	1D 37	NH 055 943
inn Giuthais or		
Creag na Feola....	1C 40	NH 133 965
inn Làir............	2F 31	NG 981 732
inn Lunndaidh.......	1C 90	NC 791 019
inn na Feusaige.....	2E 17	NH 093 542
inn na h-Eaglaise...	5F 27	NG 908 523
inn nan Màn Bàn....	3F 37	NH 108 908
inn nan Cabag.......	1F 13	NH 353 669
inn nan Cnaimhseag		
....	2F 45	NC 274 177
inn nan Coireag.....	3D 85	ND 120 254
inn nan Gearran.....	6B 92	NH 732 805
inn Poll an Tobair..	4C 48	NC 076 273
inn Ràtha...........	6F 67	NC 954 613
inn Ràtha Bheag.....	6F 67	NC 954 619
inn Rèidh...........	5D 47	NC 211 212
inn Ruadh...........	6F 65	NC 844 598
inn Ruadh...........	5D 67	NC 926 631
inn Smeòrail........	1A 88	NC 862 116
inn Spionnaidh......	4F 55	NC 362 572
inn Tarsuinn........	2A 42	NC 119 050
inn Tharsuinn Chaol		
....	1F 31	NG 989 744
en-a-Chielt.........	1B 82	ND 193 374
en-Damph Forest....	5F 27	NG 903 532
en Ainnie...........	4D 65	NC 806 649
en Arnaboll.........	3E 59	NC 459 590
en Auskaird.........	1D 51	NC 210 402
en Bhraggie.........	1C 90	NC 808 012
en Bhraggie Wood ...	1D 91	NC 824 015
en Blandy...........	4A 62	NC 625 601
en Dreavie..........	2F 51	NC 259 397
en Heilam...........	2E 59	NC 469 617
en Shieldaig........	5B 26	NG 833 524
en Strome...........	3F 51	NC 246 360
en Tongue...........	4F 61	NC 604 588
rriedale Water......	4C 84	ND 107 246
rry Hill............	6B 72	ND 238 655
ttyhill.............	3E 63	NC 706 620
Bidein a' Ghlas Thuill....	6D 37	NH 069 843
Birch Wood................	3C 8	NH 512 495
Birkle Hill...............	6F 71	ND 203 657
Bishop Kinkell............	2E 9	NH 545 528
Bishop Kinkell Woods		
....	1E 9	NH 543 530
Black Hill................	6C 74	NH 382 693
Black Hill................	1F 83	ND 263 367
Black Hill................	6C 90	NH 801 913
Black Hill................	1E 99	NH 569 634
Black Isle Brewing Company		
....	1C 6	NH 619 513
Blackmuir Wood............	4A 98	NH 486 571
Black Wood................	2E 7	NH 659 499
Blackwood.................	4D 19	NG 954 436
Blairninich...............	3A 98	NH 494 592
Blandy....................	4A 62	NC 620 599
Blàr na Coille............	5D 9	NH 538 450
Blarnalearoch.............	4C 40	NH 147 907
Blàr nam Fiadhag..........	5F 47	NC 255 206
Blood Mocc................	1D 83	ND 223 379
Bloody Moss...............	3F 71	ND 206 725
Boars of Duncansby........	3C 74	ND 379 749
Bogallan..................	1D 7	NH 636 502
Bogallan Wood.............	1E 7	NH 641 505
Boor Hill.................	1D 33	NG 837 810
Borgue....................	3E 85	ND 131 254
Bottacks..................	3A 98	NH 489 600
Boursa Island.............	2D 65	NC 808 673
Brachlach Hill............	4E 65	NC 817 638
Brae......................	3C 98	NH 523 601
Braehungie................	1B 82	ND 180 370
Braemore..................	1B 84	ND 077 298
Braemore Forest...........	6F 39	NH 220 766
Braemore Wood.............	4E 39	NH 198 802
Brae of Balnabeen.........	5F 99	NH 589 550
Brae of Easter Kinkell	1F 9	NH 577 541
Braes of Ullapool.........	3C 40	NH 142 932
Braetongue................	4F 61	NC 598 576
Braeval...................	3C 88	NC 918 082
Brahan Wood...............	5B 98	NH 503 555
Braigh na h-Eaglaise	5A 84	ND 064 220
Bràigh na Leitire.........	6D 15	NH 191 524
Bramberry Hill............	5B 88	NC 895 049
Breabag...................	3F 45	NC 286 157
Bridgepark Wood...........	2A 8	NH 464 511
Briga Head................	1E 71	ND 183 753
Brimms/Brims Ness;		
The Bowl The Cove		
& The Point..........	2D 69	ND 045 715
Brims Hill................	2F 69	ND 078 706
Broadhaven................	4D 79	ND 379 512
Broad Wood................	1D 9	NH 523 546
Broomhill.................	5A 94	NH 716 714
Brora.....................	5C 88	NC 904 039
Brora Golf Club...........	5C 88	NC 911 049
Brough....................	2A 72	ND 221 736
Bruachrobie...............	5B 88	NC 888 042
Bruthach na Garbh Choille		
....	1A 38	NH 122 852
Buldoo....................	4B 68	NC 999 672
Bulno.....................	4A 82	ND 164 307
Bunchrew..................	4C 6	NH 616 455
Bunchrew Caravan Park		
....	4C 6	NH 618 458
Burifa' Hill..............	1F 71	ND 201 755
Burnside..................	2C 96	NH 642 695
Burnt Hill................	5D 75	ND 396 707
Burrigill.................	2D 83	ND 227 344
Cadha Mòr................	3D 35	NG 943 889
Caen Hill.................	2C 86	ND 021 186
Cairn Hill................	2B 74	ND 355 768
Cairnmore Hillock.........	4E 69	ND 056 674
Cairn of Get..............	3C 80	ND 313 410
Caisteal Liath............	6A 46	NC 153 183
Caisteal Mòr.............	4F 31	NG 987 694
Caithness Broch Centre		
....	3C 76	ND 365 638
Calbha Beag...............	3A 50	NC 156 367
Calbhach Coire............	4E 55	NC 349 567
Caledonian Canal..........	6D 7	NH 625 407
Calrossie Woods...........	2E 95	NH 795 789
Camas Ruadh...............	4A 26	NG 811 559
Cambuscurrie Bay..........	4A 92	NH 724 853
Cam Loch..................	4B 44	NC 209 137
Camore....................	1D 93	NH 777 903
Camore Wood...............	2D 93	NH 774 896
Camusnagaul...............	3D 37	NH 065 892
Camustiel.................	6D 23	NG 708 421
Canisbay..................	4A 74	ND 348 721
Canisp....................	1B 44	NC 203 187
Caol Raineach.............	2A 62	NC 623 638
Càrn a' Bhaid Rabhain		
....	2F 35	NG 970 914
Càrn a' Bhiorain........	2B 38	NH 140 836
Càrn a' Bhreabadair....	2A 38	NH 112 835
Càrn a' Chaorainn......	5D 15	NH 193 544
Càrn Airigh an Easain..	6A 36	NH 002 837
Càrn Bàn...............	5B 40	NH 127 897
Càrn an Daraich........	5C 10	NH 416 578
Càrn an Eich Dheirg....	1F 33	NG 873 820
Càrn an Fharraidh......	2C 38	NG 973 904
Càrn an Fheidh.........	3A 62	NC 627 621
Càrn an Inbhire........	5C 14	NH 163 552
Càrn an Leanaidh.......	6E 15	NH 211 537
Càrn an Lochain Duibh		
....	3E 35	NG 962 889
Càrnan Maire..........	1D 31	NG 932 744
Càrn an Ruidh Mhaoil...	5D 35	NG 935 857
Càrn an Teas..........	2F 35	NG 974 901
Càrn Bad na h-Achlaise		
....	5B 34	NG 903 854
Carn Bad nan Cuileag ...	4E 35	NG 953 869
Carn Beag................	1F 17	NH 108 555
Càrn Breac............	2C 16	NH 045 530
Càrn Breac Beag........	4D 39	NH 175 795
Càrn Breac Meadhanach		
....	4C 38	NH 166 802
Càrn Breac Mòr........	4C 38	NH 160 809
Càrn Cadha an Eididh ..	2B 18	NG 914 472
Càrn Chailein..........	5A 20	NG 765 395
Càrn Chàiseachain.....	4A 12	NH 251 600
Carn Cruinn.............	5C 12	NH 290 594
Càrn Daraich..........	1F 15	NH 232 631
Càrn Dearg............	2B 20	NG 782 450
Càrn Dearg............	2C 38	NH 162 839
Carn Dearg Youth Hostel		
....	3A 32	NG 763 776
Càrn Dhòmhnuill		
Mhic a' Ghobha	5F 29	NH 026 570
Càrn Dubh.............	5B 12	NH 267 597
Carnegie Club, The......	2B 92	NH 733 892
Càrn Eite.............	1F 19	NG 999 499
Càrn Faire nan Con	4B 10	NH 395 591
Càrn Fearna...........	3D 11	NH 422 614
Càrn Garbh............	5C 12	NH 281 584
Càrn Geuradainn.......	6F 19	NG 980 398
Càrn Glac nam Fiadh ...	2D 13	NH 311 644
Càrn Gòraig...........	5A 36	NG 997 860
Càrn Gorm.............	2D 11	NH 438 629
Càrn Leum Niall.......	2F 35	NG 983 905
Carn Loch a' Choire Dhuibh		
....	6C 12	NH 282 567
Carn Loch an Tuirc.....	2D 11	NH 421 627
Càrn Loisgte..........	5F 29	NH 034 577
Càrn Mhartuin.........	5C 14	NH 174 544
Càrn Mhic Ruairidh....	3C 38	NH 161 819
Càrn Mòr.............	6B 16	NH 027 459
Càrn Mòr.............	3F 19	NG 989 446
Càrn Mòr.............	2C 62	NC 660 640
Càrn na Bèiste........	2C 12	NH 280 648
Càrn na Bèiste........	3A 36	NG 995 896
Càrn na Craoibhe-Caorunn		
....	6C 34	NG 913 823
Carn na Crè...........	5D 13	NH 306 590
Carn na Doire Duibhe ...	2F 35	NG 975 909
Carn na Fèith-Rabhain		
....	4F 15	NH 224 573
Càrn na Feòla.........	1F 27	NG 915 612
Càrn na Glaic Buidhe...	1F 35	NG 989 923
Càrn na h-Aire........	2E 35	NG 965 912
Càrn na h-Uamhaig	3B 62	NC 648 625
Càrn nam Buailtean.....	4A 36	NH 008 872
Càrn nam Fèithean	5A 38	NH 113 788
Càrn nam Fiadh........	4D 21	NG 838 412
Càrn nan Con-easan.....	4F 35	NG 987 874
Càrn na Sispein.......	2C 38	NH 158 843
Carn Odhar.............	4A 16	NH 006 496
Càrn Ruairidh.........	6D 19	NG 945 390
Carse of Bayfield......	4F 95	NH 812 734
Castle and Gardens		
of Mey, The...........	2E 73	ND 290 738
Castle Hill............	6C 8	NH 509 436
Castle Hill............	3D 9	NH 527 496
Castle Hill............	5B 88	NC 895 036
Castlehill Heritage Centre		
....	5F 71	ND 194 686
Castle of Old Wick.....	5C 78	ND 368 487
Castletown.............	5F 71	ND 196 678
Cat Hill...............	3B 96	NH 610 676
Ceann Beag.............	6A 30	NG 882 644
Ceann Caol Beinn a' Chaisgein		
....	5E 35	NG 960 849
Ceann Loch Iù.........	3F 29	NH 029 619
Ceann na h-Agh........	4A 82	ND 178 305
Cearcall Dubh..........	4E 21	NG 856 414

Chapel Hill .... 3D **95** NH 777 761
Charleston .... 2E **7** NH 643 485
Charlestown .... 5C **32** NG 811 747
Christan Hill .... 5B **74** NH 355 702
Cìoch Beinn an Eòin .. 2B **42** NC 122 065
Cìoch Mhòr .... 4F **55** NC 351 575
Cìoch Mhòr .... 1B **98** NH 503 635
Citadel .... 3F **7** NH 665 462
Clach Bheag na Faraid
.... 1C **56** NC 396 711
Clach Mhòr na Faraid ... 1C **56** NC 396 711
Clachnaharry .... 3E **7** NH 648 465
Clais-cairn Hill .... 2E **85** ND 136 275
Clais an Easaidh .... 2B **48** NC 054 308
Clais Chàrnach .... 3B **34** NH 891 880
Clan Gunn Heritage Centre
& Museum .... 3C **82** ND 202 330
Clardon Hill .... 4C **70** ND 149 695
Clashaidy .... 2C **62** NC 664 635
Clashandorran .... 4C **8** NH 515 483
Clashclevan .... 3C **62** NC 659 629
Clashmore .... 2A **48** NC 031 314
Clashmore .... 2B **92** NH 747 896
Clashmore Wood .... 1B **92** NH 739 909
Clashnessie .... 2B **48** NC 054 308
Clash Wood .... 2C **8** NH 507 514
Cliff Hill .... 2E **33** NG 850 800
Clynelish Moss .... 5B **88** NC 880 048
Clynelish Muir .... 5B **88** NC 888 047
Clyth .... 6A **80** ND 276 361
Cnap na Feola .... 5F **15** NH 228 540
Cnoc a' Bhagh Ghainmhich
.... 4C **52** NC 192 462
Cnoc a' Bhaid-rallaich.. 1D **37** NH 066 930
Cnoc a' Bhaid Shalaich
.... 4E **53** NC 226 463
Cnoc a' Bhainne .... 2A **46** NC 151 273
Cnoc a' Bhainne .... 5C **48** NC 071 257
Cnoc a' Bhodaich .... 4F **65** NC 849 631
Cnoc a' Bhraghad .... 4A **56** NC 350 657
Cnoc a' Bhreac-achaidh
.... 5C **62** NC 654 573
Cnoc a' Bhreacaich .... 2D **99** NH 544 624
Cnoc a' Bhuiridh .... 1A **98** NH 491 632
Cnoc a' Bhùthain .... 5A **52** NC 156 440
Cnoc Achadh nan Cleireach
.... 1C **10** NH 405 649
Cnoc a' Chàirn .... 5E **49** NC 113 243
Cnoc a' Chàirn Deirg .. 3A **32** NG 764 778
Cnoc a' Chàise .... 5B **52** NC 174 430
Cnoc a' Chaisteil .... 3E **41** NH 188 921
Cnoc a' Chinn .... 4B **6** NH 596 454
Cnoc a' Chlamhain .... 5D **45** NC 233 116
Cnoc a' Chlamhain .... 5B **48** NC 057 244
Cnoc a' Chlamhain .... 5E **49** NC 100 248
Cnoc a' Chlàr-locha ... 3C **52** NC 190 473
Cnoc a' Choilich .... 5D **43** NH 179 995
Cnoc a' Choilich .... 2E **47** NC 234 270
Cnoc a' Choilich Beag.. 6B **44** NC 208 097
Cnoc a' Choilich Mòr .. 6C **44** NC 211 097
Cnoc a' Choin Deirg ... 5F **49** NC 134 240
Cnoc a' Choire Bhig ... 5B **66** NC 880 637
Cnoc a' Choire Mhoir ... 5B **66** NC 880 637
Cnoc a' Chonaisg .... 5B **10** NH 390 564
Cnoc a' Chrochaire..... 3F **29** NH 026 624
Cnoc a' Chuail .... 6D **59** NC 441 526
Cnoc a' Chuilbh .... 5C **64** NC 772 613
Cnoc a' Ghairdein ...... 3B **96** NH 618 687
Cnoc a' Gharbh Doire
.... 2F **49** NC 121 304
Cnoc a' Ghille Chlais .. 5C **48** NC 079 250
Cnoc a' Ghille Shùilich
.... 5D **49** NC 083 243
Cnoc a' Ghlasraich .... 4B **66** NC 872 647
Cnoc a' Ghlinnein...... 4B **46** NC 170 239
Cnoc a' Ghrianain Beag
.... 3C **48** NC 072 291
Cnoc a' Ghrianain Mòr
.... 3C **48** NC 069 294
Cnoc Àird na Faoilinn .. 5A **52** NC 142 443
Cnoc Àird na Seilge.... 3B **46** NC 173 249
Cnoc Àirigh a' Bhraighe
.... 6D **49** NC 098 239
Cnoc Àirigh an Rathaid
.... 2D **49** NC 097 318
Cnoc Àirigh na Beinne
.... 6E **51** NC 227 308
Cnoc Airigh na Meinne
.... 6A **62** NC 624 556
Cnoc a' Mhadaidh ..... 6D **55** NC 325 525
Cnoc a' Mheirlich .... 3C **48** NC 069 285
Cnoc a' Mhill Dheirg .. 3A **48** NC 028 292
Cnoc a' Mhuilinn ...... 2B **48** NC 059 305
Cnoc a' Mhuilinn ...... 6D **49** NC 098 233

Cnoc a' Mhuilinn.......... 1D **53** NC 216 515
Cnoc a' Mhuilinn.......... 2B **98** NH 516 622
Cnoc a' Mhuilinn-Thairbh
.... 5A **98** NH 496 553
Cnoc an Achadh .... 6D **67** NC 914 612
Cnoc an Airbhe........... 2E **61** NC 584 618
Cnoc an Àite Mhòir .... 5D **49** NC 094 242
Cnoc an Aodainn .... 1D **49** NC 094 323
Cnoc an Arbhair .... 5C **62** NC 668 576
Cnoc an Arbhair .... 1A **84** NC 056 304
Cnoc an Daimh........... 5B **52** NC 160 435
Cnoc an Daimh........... 1E **53** NC 228 522
Cnoc an Daraich .... 4C **88** NC 902 062
Cnoc an Deilignidh .... 2B **96** NH 612 695
Cnoc an Droighinn ..... 5C **40** NH 148 887
Cnoc an Dubh-locha... 3D **61** NC 556 598
Cnoc an Dubharlainn... 3E **49** NC 119 281
Cnoc an Dubh Chathair
.... 2A **94** NH 716 787
Cnoc an Easain .... 5B **32** NG 782 736
Cnoc an Easain .... 3B **48** NC 050 297
Cnoc an Easain .... 5A **54** NC 260 541
Cnoc an Eòin .... 4D **53** NC 204 456
Cnoc an Fheòir .... 1F **53** NC 256 528
Cnoc an Fheòir .... 5A **54** NC 258 542
Cnoc an Fhir Bhreige .. 1A **50** NC 147 419
Cnoc an Fhir Bhreige .. 2B **52** NC 172 501
Cnoc an Fhreiceadain .. 3D **55** NC 324 598
Cnoc an Fhreiceadain .. 4A **62** NC 611 594
Cnoc an Fhuarain....... 4D **53** NC 200 460
Cnoc an Leathaid Bhain
.... 5A **54** NC 251 554
Cnoc an Leathaid Bhig
.... 3C **44** NC 228 142
Cnoc an Leathaid Bhuidhe
.... 3D **45** NC 231 153
Cnoc an Leòid .... 1A **96** NH 592 719
Cnoc an Leòthaid ...... 2A **48** NC 038 317
Cnoc an Leòthaid ...... 4A **46** NC 144 233
Cnoc an Leothaid Bhuidhe
.... 4C **46** NC 185 230
Cnoc an Locha Chròcaich
.... 3E **49** NC 102 281
Cnoc an Lochain Dhuibh
.... 2F **49** NC 132 311
Cnoc an Lochain Fheòir
.... 3E **47** NC 229 249
Cnoc an Lochain Sgeirich
.... 5C **48** NC 069 254
Cnoc an Lòin Bhàin .... 1F **53** NC 243 511
Cnoc an Loisgein ...... 1B **62** NC 638 656
Cnoc an Ràth .... 5D **9** NH 522 465
Cnoc an Rathaid Mhòir
.... 4E **65** NC 813 647
Cnoc an Ruadhlaich ... 4B **44** NC 208 126
Cnoc an Ruffer .... 5A **66** NC 851 637
Cnoc an Ruighe Dhorcha
.... 6B **50** NC 168 307
Cnoc an Sasannaich ... 1E **43** NC 192 087
Cnoc an Sgaid .... 5B **32** NG 785 745
Cnoc an Sgaid .... 5A **52** NC 763 740
Cnoc an Sgrìodaich .... 3C **48** NC 062 294
Cnoc an t-Sabhail ...... 4C **32** NG 808 765
Cnoc an t-Sabhail ...... 5D **50** NC 174 409
Cnoc an t-Sabhail ...... 2B **52** NC 175 499
Cnoc an t-Sabhail ...... 6A **92** NH 721 817
Cnoc an t-Seagail....... 4D **45** NC 243 135
Cnoc an t-Seallaidh ... 4C **46** NC 198 233
Cnoc an t-Sean-bhaile
.... 5B **32** NG 787 742
Cnoc an t-Sean Eòin ... 1F **49** NC 126 331
Cnoc an t-Sithean ...... 6B **14** NH 151 539
Cnoc an t-Sithean ...... 4B **48** NC 050 279
Cnoc an t-Sratha......... 6D **19** NG 942 386
Cnoc an Taghain......... 5C **48** NC 064 249
Cnoc an Taigh Choinneimh
.... 5D **49** NC 091 243
Cnoc an Tearnaidh ..... 2A **10** NH 361 630
Cnoc an Teine .... 4A **8** NH 469 471
Cnoc an Tighe .... 4A **62** NC 617 608
Cnoc an Tolla Bhaid ... 6E **49** NC 110 235
Cnoc an Tubhadair..... 2E **87** ND 050 187
Cnoc an Tùir .... 6A **54** NC 252 534
Cnoc an Uillt Tharsuinn
.... 1A **60** NC 508 633
Cnoc a' Phobuill .... 2C **62** NC 663 637
Cnoc à' Phollain Bheithe
.... 1D **49** NC 092 322
Cnoc a' Phreasain Challtuinne
.... 4C **52** NC 188 468
Cnoc a' Phuillachair ... 4D **63** NC 672 608
Cnoc Ardoch .... 1A **96** NH 609 725
Cnoc Aulaidh............. 3A **98** NH 480 593
Cnoc Bad a' Baine ...... 5E **49** NC 109 245

Cnoc Bad a' Chrasgaidh
.... 1A **90** NC 754 0?
Cnoc Bad an Aon Tighe
.... 1E **49** NC 114 3?
Cnoc Badan na h-Earbaige
.... 2C **34** NG 924 9?
Cnoc Bad Asgaraidh .. 5B **84** ND 085 2?
Cnoc Bad na Clèithe ... 3D **45** NC 240 1?
Cnoc Bad na Conaire .. 5E **49** NC 109 2?
Cnoc Bad na Goibhre .. 6C **48** NC 074 2?
Cnoc Bad na Goibhre .. 6E **49** NC 106 2?
Cnoc Bad na h-Achlaise
.... 5D **45** NC 241 1?
Cnoc Bad na h-Achlaise
.... 5F **53** NC 246 4.
Cnoc Bad nan Aighean
.... 5F **49** NC 129 2?
Cnoc Bad nan Cuileag
.... 3D **35** NG 949 8?
Cnoc Bàgh a' Choit ..... 3C **52** NC 181 4?
Cnoc Ban .... 5C **18** NG 932 4?
Cnoc Bàn .... 2E **15** NH 219 6?
Cnoc Beag .... 4B **48** NC 048 2?
Cnoc Bealach na Mòine
.... 2B **52** NC 176 5?
Cnoc Bealach nam Piob
.... 4B **52** NC 168 4?
Cnoc Bealach nan Corr
.... 5A **98** NH 490 5?
Cnoc Beinn na Lice .... 3A **8** NH 469 4?
Cnoc Bhair .... 6A **90** NH 761 9?
Cnoc Bioraiche .... 5A **50** NC 145 3?
Cnoc Bioraig .... 4B **48** NC 048 2?
Cnoc Braonach .... 6D **49** NC 083 2?
Cnoc Breac .... 1B **40** NH 119 9?
Cnoc Breac .... 5C **44** NC 217 1?
Cnoc Breac .... 2E **47** NC 233 2?
Cnoc Breac .... 4A **48** NC 030 2?
Cnoc Breac .... 3A **82** ND 162 3?
Cnoc Breac .... 3A **96** NH 595 6?
Cnoc Buidhe .... 5A **8** NH 474 4?
Cnoc Buidhe .... 5B **32** NG 787 7?
Cnoc Cadha an Airbhe
.... 4B **48** NC 049 2?
Cnoc Cailleach Iain .... 2E **65** NC 134 3?
Cnoc Caol .... 2E **65** NC 818 6?
Cnoc Càrn a' Bhodaich
.... 1D **53** NC 217 5?
Cnoc Chalbha .... 2C **50** NC 180 3?
Cnoc Chluaine .... 6A **8** NH 468 4?
Cnoc Chorkael .... 6C **66** NC 895 6?
Cnoc Clais an Uisge ... 5A **52** NC 153 4?
Cnoc Coillteil .... 6F **65** NC 835 5?
Cnoc Coir' a' Bhaic..... 1F **47** NC 241 2?
Cnoc Coir' a' Phuill .... 1D **87** ND 046 2?
Cnoc Corr .... 2D **53** NC 217 5?
Cnoc Còrr .... 5A **52** NC 144 4?
Cnoc Cragaidh .... 2A **88** NC 861 1?
Cnoc Creagach .... 3E **11** NH 446 6?
Cnoc Creag an Spardain
.... 5E **51** NC 220 3?
Cnoc Croit na Maoile .. 3B **8** NH 491 4?
Cnoc Dabhaich .... 6D **49** NC 080 2?
Cnoc Dachow............. 4F **67** NC 963 6?
Cnoc Dail a' Chairn .... 5A **62** NC 624 5?
Cnoc Daimh .... 2A **16** NH 008 5?
Cnoc Daimh .... 5D **49** NC 088 2?
Cnoc Daimh .... 3D **49** NC 098 2?
Cnoc Daimh .... 5B **50** NC 174 3?
Cnoc Dalveghouse ..... 6F **63** NC 711 5?
Cnoc Damh .... 5C **56** NC 401 6?
Cnoc Doire Beathaig... 3A **46** NC 150 2?
Cnoc Donn .... 2E **29** NH 012 6?
Cnoc Donn a' Phris .... 1F **43** NC 210 0?
Cnoc Druim na Coille .. 2C **52** NC 191 4?
Cnoc Dubh .... 4A **8** NH 467 4?
Cnoc Dubh .... 6C **10** NH 404 5?
Cnoc Dubh .... 4D **11** NH 438 5?
Cnoc Dubh .... 5E **21** NG 844 3?
Cnoc Dubh .... 4E **41** NH 172 9?
Cnoc Dubh .... 2C **60** NC 542 6?
Cnoc Dubh .... 3E **65** NC 814 6?
Cnoc Dubh .... 5A **98** NH 490 5?
Cnoc Dubh a' Bhlàir Mhòine
.... 3E **13** NH 326 6?
Cnoc Dubh-chadha ..... 6C **58** NC 427 5?
Cnoc Dubh an Ruighe Ruaidh
.... 2A **10** NH 364 6?
Cnoc Dubh Dothaig..... 4F **47** NC 248 2?
Cnoc Dubh Mòr .... 4F **47** NC 257 2?
Cnoc Dubh Ùidh nan Caorach
.... 5D **45** NC 234 1?
Cnoc Duchaire .... 1B **96** NH 617 7?
Cnoc Dùin .... 1D **85** NH 114 2?

Cnoc Eadar Dha Allt – Coire Crubaidh

oc Eadar Dha Allt 4A **66** NC 867 644
oc Eilean nan Gall 4D **63** NC 681 605
oc Eilid Mhathain 1F **45** NC 278 183
oc Eilig 2D **61** NC 553 618
oc Eipteil 5A **66** NC 864 628
oc Falaisge 5E **51** NC 231 331
oc Feàrna 5F **65** NC 839 612
oc Fionn 4C **84** ND 106 237
oc Freiceadain 5C **68** ND 012 653
oc Fyrish 2A **96** NH 607 697
oc Garbh 4D **51** NC 214 355
oc Garbh 2C **52** NC 194 508
oc Geal 4D **13** NH 309 611
oc Geal 3F **65** NC 840 656
oc Glac na Goibhre 4D **49** NC 082 263
oc Glac na h-Imrich 4D **49** NC 088 260
oc Glac na Stàirne 1D **53** NC 210 528
oc Glas 3B **18** NG 901 458
oc Glas 3E **65** NC 811 666
oc Glas 2F **65** NC 830 680
oc Glas 4D **67** NC 928 656
oc Glas Blàr nam Fiadhag 5F **47** NC 257 203
oc Gleannan nan Caorach 6D **51** NC 214 317
oc Gorm 6E **45** NC 259 087
oc Gorm 4F **47** NC 258 225
oc Gorm 2B **52** NC 167 498
oc Heara 4B **82** ND 180 315
oc Iseabail 2A **34** NG 874 911
oc Leathan 2E **49** NC 118 319
oc Leathan 2F **53** NC 256 507
oc Leathann 5C **56** NC 391 633
oc Liath 6C **44** NC 227 080
oc Lochan na Bà Ruaidhe 2C **52** NC 180 490
oc Lochan na Creige 3C **48** NC 071 284
oc Lochan na Seanaig 3D **61** NC 563 603
oc Lòn nan Eildean 4C **60** NC 542 572
oc Maovally 3A **60** NC 507 609
oc Meadhonach 1A **86** NC 982 209
oc Mhàbairn 1D **99** NH 559 638
oc Mhichie 4B **52** NC 172 465
oc Mòine a' Ghuail 1B **40** NH 112 978
oc Mòr 6D **21** NG 838 368
oc Mòr 4B **48** NC 050 264
oc Mòr 4B **64** NC 756 637
oc Mòr 5A **98** NH 490 569
oc na Bagh Choille 5B **50** NC 179 338
oc na Bainnse 2A **98** NH 493 619
oc na Banaraich 6A **52** NC 155 427
oc na Bantraich 5A **68** NC 979 645
oc na Broige 2E **49** NC 112 313
oc na Buaile 1B **48** NC 046 326
oc na Buaile 5A **52** NC 147 444
oc na Caillich 2E **35** NG 959 903
oc na Caillich 1B **62** NC 644 655
oc na Cailliche 4A **66** NC 864 648
oc na Cainach 4B **80** ND 309 402
oc na Cairidh 5E **51** NC 228 326
oc na Caorach Glaise 5A **52** NC 157 438
oc na Ciste 2D **49** NC 081 310
oc na Comhlaich 2C **46** NC 190 265
oc na Crask 2A **82** ND 165 345
oc na Creige 3A **18** NG 884 449
oc na Creige 1F **47** NC 259 289
oc na Creige 5C **48** NC 061 249
oc na Croiche 2C **40** NH 138 946
oc na Croiche 3E **63** NC 706 615
oc na Croiche 4A **82** ND 173 316
oc na Croiche 5C **84** ND 106 211
oc na Croiche 2E **91** NC 844 004
oc na Croiche 3D **95** NH 774 756
oc na Cròige 3B **96** NH 626 683
oc na Cuthaige 2B **52** NC 166 493
oc na Dalach Baite 4E **65** NC 828 640
oc na Doire Tarsuinn 5C **50** NC 182 333
oc na Droighniche 4E **49** NC 116 269
oc na Dubh-chlaise 6D **65** NC 806 598
oc na Feadaige 3F **69** ND 070 690
oc na Feadaige 1C **84** ND 099 294
oc na Gaoithe 5A **14** NH 137 554
oc na Gaoithe 2D **29** NG 991 646
oc na Gaoithe 4C **44** NC 227 123
oc na Gaoithe 2A **96** NH 600 704
oc na Gearraisich 2F **11** NH 473 625
oc na Glaic Duinne 6D **49** NC 088 233
oc na Glaice Mòire 5C **52** NC 184 448
oc na Glaodhaich 4E **11** NH 457 594
Cnoc na Glas-Choille 6F **45** NC 276 080
Cnoc na h-Airbhe 6F **49** NC 128 232
Cnoc na h-Àtha 6C **18** NG 928 388
Cnoc na h-Àtha 3C **18** NG 935 457
Cnoc na h-Eaglaise 6B **52** NC 167 420
Cnoc na h-Earra 5F **35** NG 986 855
Cnoc na h-Eilde 3D **19** NG 955 452
Cnoc na h-Eilde 2A **48** NC 024 313
Cnoc na h-Iolaire 1A **10** NH 367 643
Cnoc na h-Iolaire 3B **10** NH 388 608
Cnoc na h-Iolaire 2D **15** NC 932 108
Cnoc na h-Iolaire 5E **41** NH 176 894
Cnoc na h-Iolaire 6B **48** NC 050 237
Cnoc na h-Iolaire 6E **49** NC 101 227
Cnoc na h-Uidhe Doimhne 3C **48** NC 070 286
Cnoc na Laitch 2D **99** NH 557 610
Cnoc na Leacaig 5A **52** NC 148 440
Cnoc na Leanaig Gile 4F **65** NC 848 649
Cnoc na Lise 1F **33** NG 863 813
Cnoc na Luibhe 1B **8** NH 406 484
Cnoc nam Ban 4A **12** NH 258 616
Cnoc nam Brac 1E **51** NC 222 413
Cnoc nam Bràigh 5E **57** NC 448 644
Cnoc nam Broc 5B **14** NH 145 557
Cnoc nam Broc 3F **21** NG 862 438
Cnoc nam Buachaillean 6F **65** NC 847 609
Cnoc nam Buaile 4C **32** NG 811 750
Cnoc nam Fiadh 2A **46** NC 140 273
Cnoc nam Meann 2E **35** NG 962 919
Cnoc nam Miar Beaga 5B **52** NC 175 446
Cnoc na Moine 5B **6** NH 597 421
Cnoc na Moine 3F **17** NH 118 517
Cnoc na Moine 4E **67** NC 939 651
Cnoc na Moine 1A **96** NH 598 726
Cnoc na Mòine 5A **8** NH 478 458
Cnoc na Mòine 4A **36** NG 998 889
Cnoc na Mòine 2E **39** NH 207 838
Cnoc na Mòine 1B **40** NH 111 961
Cnoc na Mòine 6C **48** NC 062 235
Cnoc na Mòine 5E **51** NC 233 328
Cnoc na Mòine 6B **52** NC 160 425
Cnoc na Mòine 6A **54** NC 260 522
Cnoc na Mòine 4B **56** NC 389 658
Cnoc na Mòine 1D **61** NC 567 641
Cnoc na Mòine 5B **98** NH 510 554
Cnoc nan Cabar 1E **49** NC 110 332
Cnoc nan Caorach 6C **48** NC 075 227
Cnoc nan Caorach 5E **51** NC 225 334
Cnoc nan Caorach 5A **98** NH 488 558
Cnoc nan Caorach Beaga 5E **49** NC 100 259
Cnoc nan Cnàmh 4B **48** NC 046 269
Cnoc nan Colunnan 3A **34** NG 884 898
Cnoc nan Cro 4F **53** NC 242 459
Cnoc nan Cuilean 1D **55** NC 328 626
Cnoc nan Doireachan Donna 5C **48** NC 062 245
Cnoc nan Each 3E **19** NG 963 458
Cnoc nan Each 5D **27** NG 876 532
Cnoc nan Each 3B **32** NG 795 785
Cnoc nan Each Beag 2F **11** NH 461 638
Cnoc nan Each Mòr 1E **11** NH 455 644
Cnoc nan Eilid 1F **19** NG 997 483
Cnoc nan Eun 3D **53** NC 216 471
Cnoc nan Gobhar 1D **35** NG 940 936
Cnoc nan Gobhar 1A **60** NC 490 631
Cnoc nan Gobhar 1E **61** NC 574 645
Cnoc nan Lochan Cuilce 3C **52** NC 193 480
Cnoc nan Ràthag 3C **52** NC 185 483
Cnoc nan Sac 5C **48** NC 063 248
Cnoc nan Sasunnach 5F **11** NH 462 571
Cnoc nan Sgliat 1B **56** NC 389 710
Cnoc nan Sguad 2E **17** NH 096 530
Cnoc nan Stalcan 5C **44** NC 212 108
Cnoc nan Uamhag 4E **57** NC 437 660
Cnoc nan Uan 5E **19** NG 972 419
Cnoc nan Uan 4F **49** NC 126 278
Cnoc nan Uan 2C **62** NC 667 631
Cnoc nan Uidhean Beaga 4D **49** NC 089 272
Cnoc nan Urchair 4D **65** NC 807 642
Cnoc na Pollaig 5A **52** NC 146 446
Cnoc na Sàile 6F **53** NC 257 426
Cnoc na Snàthaid 2A **82** ND 163 343
Cnoc na Sròine 4E **45** NC 254 128
Cnoc na Staing 5B **18** NG 906 405
Cnoc na Stri 2E **87** ND 067 183
Cnoc na Stròine 4E **45** NC 254 128
Cnoc na Sùil Chruthaiche 1D **53** NC 205 511
Cnoc na Suileig 2C **48** NC 066 314
Cnoc na Tobaireach 6E **67** NC 933 613
Cnoc na Tuthcaid 3F **65** NC 843 650
Cnoc Navie 1D **97** NH 661 724
Cnoc Neill Dhuinn 6B **52** NC 163 426
Cnoc Odhar 6A **50** NC 141 307
Cnoc Odhar 2E **51** NC 220 383
Cnoc Odhar 1D **61** NC 560 644
Cnoc Odhar 4A **90** NH 757 966
Cnoc Odhar an Teanrich 6A **50** NC 144 306
Cnoc Phadruig 3F **41** NH 199 928
Cnoc Poll a' Mhuilt 3A **48** NC 031 292
Cnoc Pollan nan Gamhna 4D **49** NC 083 278
Cnoc Poll an Turrabain 2B **52** NC 163 494
Cnoc Poll Dhaidh 3C **48** NC 077 284
Cnoc Poll nam Muc 3A **46** NC 152 255
Cnoc Raon na Ceardaich 6D **40** NC 000 255
Cnoc Ravoch 2D **99** NH 557 613
Cnoc Rèile 2A **82** ND 165 345
Cnoc Riabhach 1A **48** NC 026 320
Cnoc Ruadh 4A **96** NH 600 663
Cnoc Rubha an Ghorbhan 3C **52** NC 183 475
Cnoc Ruigh a' Chàirn 2B **48** NC 046 314
Cnoc Ruigh a' Chlachain 5C **48** NC 079 244
Cnoc Ruigh Thulaich 4D **45** NC 235 127
Cnoc Seònaid 3D **65** NC 803 650
Cnoc Sheangan 3A **82** ND 162 332
Cnoc Sheumais 5B **8** NH 485 466
Cnoc Sloc a' Bhuilg 5E **49** NC 101 242
Cnoc Spàrdain 4B **84** ND 078 233
Cnoc Sròn a Mhartuinn 1D **61** NC 557 649
Cnoc Taigh Adhamh 3B **52** NC 170 488
Cnoc Thormaid 6C **52** NC 189 424
Cnoc Thull 2F **53** NC 246 494
Cnoc Tigh na Fhirich 2D **99** NH 553 624
Cnoc Toiteach 5D **61** NC 557 563
Cnoc Udais 3B **8** NH 480 498
Cnoc Uidh na Geadaig 5F **49** NC 135 251
Coigach 2B **42** NC 130 067
Coill' an Achaidh Mhòir 3C **10** NH 415 600
Coill' an Righe 4C **98** NH 524 588
Coille an t-Seana-Mhorair 5E **27** NG 883 538
Coille Bhàn 3D **17** NH 060 521
Coille Bheag 1B **10** NH 394 651
Coille Bhreac 3D **17** NH 073 525
Coille Braigh na h-Eaglaise 5B **84** ND 071 227
Coille Cnoc na h-Eireachd 2D **7** NH 622 495
Coille Coire Mhuilidh 2A **10** NH 364 626
Coille Creag-Loch 5B **26** NG 824 521
Coille Duasdal Beag 4E **43** NC 186 016
Coille Fearna 5A **10** NH 362 561
Coille Gharbh 4E **37** NH 071 881
Coille Mhòr 4E **11** NH 450 583
Coille Mhòr 4D **33** NG 822 751
Coille Mhoruisge 3F **17** NH 106 526
Coille na Cleithe 5A **8** NH 467 450
Coille na Glas-Leitire 2E **29** NH 002 645
Coille na h-Inghinn 5D **33** NG 823 747
Coille Riabach 3E **9** NH 544 500
Coille Uisge 1A **8** NH 470 546
Còinneach Mhòr 4B **28** NG 944 600
Coir' a' Bhaid-Choill 3B **36** NH 024 902
Coir' a' Ghuibhsachain 6F **37** NH 095 837
Coir' Allt a' Choin Idhir 1F **11** NH 479 651
Coir' an Eich Ghlais 5A **38** NH 122 784
Coir' an Taoibh Riabhaich 2E **31** NG 968 735
Coire a' Bhàinidh 5B **16** NH 035 475
Coire a' Chaorachain 3B **20** NG 794 422
Coire an Laoigh 6E **27** NG 897 502
Coire an t-Seilich 4D **17** NH 077 495
Coire an Uinnseinn 5F **55** NC 359 558
Coire Bad Asgaraidh 5B **84** ND 089 221
Coire Beinn Làir 2F **31** NG 974 724
Coire Beithe 5F **17** NH 113 488
Coire Broige 4F **31** NG 989 697
Coire Carn Earachain 6C **36** NH 036 841
Coire Crom 1D **37** NH 069 942
Coire Cronaidh 3F **41** NH 207 924
Coire Crubaidh 3C **16** NH 056 529

Coire Dearg................1D **37** NH 054 946
Coire Doire Aonair........6A **26** NG 806 514
Coire Donn................6A **34** NG 881 839
Coire Dubh................6F **15** NH 222 530
Coire Dubh................3D **41** NH 167 936
Coire Dubh................2E **45** NC 258 162
Coire Dubh Mòr...........5B **28** NG 948 589
Coire Earba...............1F **19** NH 994 487
Coire Garbh..............1C **18** NG 932 495
Coire Glas...............3E **23** NG 728 484
Coire Leathad an Tobair
........................6D **17** NH 064 452
Coire Liath..............5F **21** NG 869 389
Coire Mac an Leasgadair
........................1F **19** NG 995 492
Coire Mhic Iomhair.......2E **13** NH 321 659
Coire MhicNòbaill........2D **27** NG 873 582
Coire Murrchaidh.........6C **26** NG 841 506
Coire Mòr an Teallaich
........................5D **37** NH 056 853
Coire na Creubhaich......6C **56** NC 393 622
Coire na Cùile...........3C **18** NG 920 450
Coire na Feàrna..........5D **27** NG 870 521
Coire na Fèithe Riabhaich
........................1E **11** NH 459 656
Coire na Feòla...........2C **20** NG 815 443
Coire na h-Uidhe.........1A **30** NG 872 756
Coire nam Bò Dubha......2E **11** NH 459 638
Coire nan Cadhan.........2B **18** NG 905 479
Coire nan Clach..........4A **20** NG 772 416
Coire nan Laogh..........2C **20** NG 859 595
Coire Rèidh..............1D **31** NG 936 754
Coire Riabhach...........1B **88** NC 898 127
Coire Roill..............6E **27** NG 894 516
Coire Sgamhadail.........5B **20** NG 781 390
Coire Taodail............4F **19** NG 992 435
Col-Bheinn...............1B **88** NC 886 110
Coldbackie...............4A **62** NC 614 599
Con-easan................4F **35** NG 989 866
Cona Chreag..............3D **49** NC 094 297
Conon Bridge.............5D **99** NH 543 555
Contin...................5E **11** NH 456 564
Contin Mountain Bike Trails
........................5E **11** NH 456 569
Cooper's Hill............6A **72** ND 218 653
Corntown.................5D **99** NH 557 560
Corriemoillie Forest.....1F **13** NH 349 670
Corrieshalloch Gorge.....5E **39** NH 200 782
Corrieshalloch Gorge National
   Nature Reserve........5E **39** NH 201 780
Corry Point..............3C **40** NH 144 923
Corry Wood...............4C **8** NH 500 483
Coul.....................2C **96** NH 645 704
Coulhill Wood............2C **96** NH 646 703
Coulwood.................5F **11** NH 477 570
Couper Hill..............3B **72** ND 232 710
Courtfall Hill...........2F **71** ND 208 742
Court Hill...............2C **94** NH 764 772
Craft Wools And Weavers
........................3B **24** NG 712 584
Craggach Wood...........5A **6** NH 570 437
Craig....................4C **16** NH 040 492
Craig Andrew.............2C **68** ND 029 704
Craig Hill...............6A **74** ND 331 698
Craigiehowe Wood........1F **7** NH 674 514
Craig Phadrig............4D **7** NH 639 452
Craigphadrig Forest......4D **7** NH 639 454
Craigrory................2D **7** NH 620 488
Craigton.................2F **7** NH 660 481
Craig Youth Hostel.......1E **25** NG 774 638
Cranstackie..............5F **55** NC 350 555
Crasbackie Hill..........4C **64** NC 778 634
Crask....................3F **63** NC 720 625
Creag-Mheall Beag........4F **35** NG 973 861
Creag-Mheall Meadhonach
........................5F **35** NG 978 841
Creag a' Bhraighe........1F **49** NC 123 320
Creag a' Chaoruinn.......4C **10** NH 407 586
Creag a' Chlàr Locha.....6D **53** NC 202 427
Creag a' Chrionaich......1D **15** NC 924 115
Creag a' Chroisg.........3C **44** NG 220 159
Creag an Amalaidh........3A **90** NH 758 975
Creagan an Eich Ghlais
........................1B **10** NH 384 643
Creagan Breac...........6B **62** NC 634 557
Creagan Breaca..........1F **45** NC 270 193
Creagan Cosach..........5B **84** ND 086 213
Creagan Dubh Toll nam Biast
........................6E **27** NG 886 510
Creag an Fhithich........6A **54** NC 257 534
Creag an Fhraoich........2A **26** NG 809 585
Creagan Mòr.............4B **44** NC 192 139
Creagan Mòr.............3C **88** NC 915 087

Creagan na Speireig.....5F **59** NC 482 549
Creagan Reamhar.........3D **85** ND 120 262
Creag an Turaraich.......1A **18** NG 883 489
Creag a' Phris...........4B **50** NC 165 345
Creag Bac na Faire.......4F **39** NH 228 807
Creag Bhreaig...........6E **59** NC 450 530
Creag Bun-Ullidh........3C **86** ND 029 155
Creag Chailein..........5B **66** NC 883 623
Creag Clais nan Cruineachd
........................4C **48** NC 067 279
Creag Dalhorrisgle.......6E **63** NC 707 560
Creag Deabharan.........6F **41** NH 205 874
Creag Dharaich..........5D **49** NC 080 257
Creag Dhonn.............6C **12** NH 289 567
Creag Dhubh.............6D **29** NG 982 567
Creag Dhubh.............4D **29** NG 983 604
Creag Dhubh.............6F **39** NH 212 760
Creag Dhubh.............1D **43** NC 162 086
Creag Dhubh.............1C **50** NC 192 406
Creag Dhubh Coille a' Bhun
........................2B **38** NH 136 839
Creag Dhubh Mhòr.......5F **19** NG 982 404
Creag Leathan...........6A **68** NC 983 631
Creag Liath.............5B **46** NC 163 212
Creag Loch nan Dearcag
........................6E **13** NH 333 567
Creag Loisgte...........4B **86** NC 996 138
Creag Mainnrichean......1E **19** NG 971 488
Creag Marail............3C **86** ND 013 161
Creag Mhòr.............2E **13** NH 325 644
Creag Mhòr.............6B **68** NC 991 625
Creag Mhòr Tholdaidh...3F **33** NG 864 776
Creag na Ceapaich.......3E **37** NH 088 896
Creag na Cuinge.........6B **84** ND 077 194
Creag na Faoilinn.......6B **58** NC 396 535
Creag na Feòl...........2B **28** NG 942 641
Creag na Fionndalach....3C **52** NC 196 486
Creag na h-Iolaire.......3A **18** NG 899 443
Creag na h-Iolaire.......6B **42** NH 137 985
Creag na h-Iolaire.......1C **46** NC 189 280
Creag na h-Uamha.......2B **24** NG 717 610
Creag nan Corrachan......4F **13** NH 346 603
Creag nan Speireag......1F **41** NH 204 974
Creag na Rianaich.......5E **29** NH 009 572
Creag Riabhach..........1D **15** NG 936 119
Creag Riabhach..........1B **54** NC 278 638
Creag Riasgain..........1E **15** NC 957 126
Creag Ruadh............2A **30** NG 874 934
Creag Ruadh............1F **59** NC 486 620
Creag Ruadh............2E **63** NC 695 630
Creag Thoraraidh........2E **87** ND 040 187
Creag Ulladail..........4F **11** NH 470 588
Croc-na-Feannaig........2E **33** NG 857 795
Croftnacriech...........2D **7** NH 633 491
Croftown................2D **39** NH 178 839
Croiche Wood............6D **9** NH 520 437
Cromalt Hills............1F **43** NC 209 070
Cromarty Firth..........6C **94** NH 757 691
Cromsac Hill............5D **65** NC 794 627
Crow Hillock............3B **76** ND 347 644
Crown...................4F **7** NH 672 452
Cùl Beag................1C **42** NC 140 088
Cùl Eilean..............1F **49** NC 124 336
Culgower Hill............4A **86** NC 974 134
Culkein Drumbeg.........1E **49** NC 113 336
Cullaird Wood...........6D **7** NH 639 405
Cullicudden.............5C **96** NH 648 638
Culmaily Plantation......2C **90** NH 808 998
Cunndainn..............5E **11** NH 456 564
Cuthill Sands............3C **92** NH 767 873

Dail Gheal..............3A **96** NH 608 675
Dail na Drochaide.......5F **63** NC 718 575
Dalchalm...............4C **88** NC 909 056
Dalcharn...............5A **62** NC 622 586
Dalmore Distillery.......3D **97** NH 662 684
Dalneigh................4E **7** NH 654 449
Dalreoch Wood..........1B **96** NH 628 726
Dell, The...............1C **8** NH 513 544
Delny..................5E **94** NH 734 723
Den, The...............5E **69** ND 062 640
Den, The...............5E **97** NH 688 640
Den Moss...............2B **82** ND 186 358
Dial Hill...............2C **62** NC 661 630
Dingwall...............4D **99** NH 551 587
District Museum, Tain
........................5D **93** NH 781 820
Diuranais..............3C **56** NC 402 677
Doire a' Chapuill.......4F **29** NH 036 609
Doire Beathaig..........3A **46** NC 149 257
Doire Beithe...........6A **28** NG 937 559
Doire Daimh...........4D **47** NC 200 235
Doire Damh............6D **27** NG 871 510

Doire Dhubh............4A **38** NH 129 7?
Doire Dhubh............6D **45** NC 235 0?
Doire Dhubh............2B **50** NC 178 3?
Doire Gharbh...........1B **14** NH 156 6?
Doire na Caillich.......3F **27** NG 919 5?
Doire na h-Achlaise.....3B **36** NH 028 9?
Doire nan Gobhar.......1C **14** NH 178 6?
Doire nan Tota.........4E **37** NH 077 8?
Doire na Saobhaidhe....6A **38** NH 129 7?
Doll...................5A **88** NC 879 0?
Dornoch...............2E **93** NH 798 8?
Dornoch Caravan &
   Camping Park........2E **93** NH 802 8?
Dornoch Cathedral......2E **93** NH 797 8?
Dornoch Craft Centre....2E **93** NH 797 8?
Dornoch Firth
   Caravan Park.........4B **92** NH 745 6?
Dornoch Sands.........3D **93** NH 786 8?
Dorrachan.............4A **94** NH 718 7?
Dos Mhucarain.........2D **15** NH 197 6?
Dosmucheran Plantation
........................3D **15** NH 192 5?
Dounreay Power Station
........................4A **68** NC 987 6?
Driemastle Wood........1C **92** NH 761 9?
Druim a' Chuilein......2A **98** NH 489 6?
Druim a' Ghiubhais......4F **13** NH 357 6?
Druim Allt a' Mhuilinn
........................2E **65** NC 820 6?
Druim Donn............1D **43** NC 174 0?
Druim Dubh............2C **34** NG 917 9?
Druim Lochan na Ba Caoile
........................1F **33** NG 873 8?
Druim na h-Imrich......4D **51** NC 204 3?
Druim nam Fuath.......1A **36** NG 996 9?
Drumbeg...............1F **49** NC 122 3?
Drumchardine..........4A **6** NH 569 4?
Drumchork.............3A **34** NG 878 8?
Drumderfit Hill.........1E **7** NH 654 5?
Drumindorsair..........5B **8** NH 488 4?
Drummond..............4A **96** NH 603 6?
Drumsmittal Plantation
........................2E **7** NH 644 4?
Drumsmittal Wood.......2E **7** NH 652 4?
Drynie Park............2E **9** NH 555 5?
Duartmore Forest.......3C **50** NC 194 3?
Dubh-Àird.............4D **27** NG 870 5?
Dubh-sgeir Mhòr.......1F **61** NC 597 6?
Duchess Countess Plantation
........................6B **90** NH 789 9?
Duel Hill..............6E **93** NH 793 8?
Dunain Hill............5D **7** NH 626 4?
Dunballoch Plantation
........................5D **9** NH 528 4?
Dunbeath..............5A **82** ND 161 2?
Dunbeath Broch........1E **85** ND 144 3?
Dunbeath Castle........2F **85** ND 157 2?
Dunbeath Water.........5A **82** ND 162 2?
Dunbeath Water.........1E **85** ND 148 3?
Duncansby Head.........4D **75** ND 403 7?
Duncansby Head Lighthouse
........................4D **75** ND 405 7?
Duncan's Hill..........5C **70** ND 137 6?
Duncanston............5F **99** NH 589 5?
Dundonnell.............4F **37** NH 094 8?
Dundonnell House.......1A **38** NH 114 8?
Dunglass Island........1D **9** NH 536 5?
Dunmore...............4C **8** NH 514 4?
Dunnet................3A **72** ND 215 7?
Dunnet Bay............4E **71** ND 184 7?
Dunnet Bay............4A **72** ND 212 7?
Dunnet Head...........1F **71** ND 205 7?
Dunnet Head Lighthouse
........................1F **71** ND 202 7?
Dunnet Hill............2F **71** ND 191 7?
Dunrobin Castle........2F **91** NC 850 0?
Dunrobin Wood.........6A **88** NC 861 0?
Durnamuck............2B **36** NH 011 9?
Durness...............3C **56** NC 402 6?
Durness/Balnakeil Bay
........................2B **56** NC 389 6?
Durness Golf Club.......3B **56** NC 384 6?
Durness Old Church, Balnakeil
........................3B **56** NC 389 6?
Durness Youth Hostel
........................3D **57** NC 416 6?
Dwarwick Head.........3F **71** ND 205 7?

Eagan.................6A **16** NH 019 4?
Eagle Stone...........4A **98** NH 484 5?
East Brora............5C **88** NC 904 0?
East Brora Muir........5C **88** NC 907 0?
East Clyne............4C **88** NC 900 0?

...ster Head	1F **71**	ND 202 766
...ster Kinkell	5E **99**	NH 576 554
...ster Lamington Wood		
	2C **94**	NH 753 786
...st Lonvine	4A **94**	NH 729 731
...st Helmsdale	3C **86**	ND 026 154
...st Raeberry	4D **71**	ND 150 702
...st Scaraben	2B **84**	ND 079 272
...st Slate	2C **68**	ND 029 707
...st Top	4A **10**	NH 369 590
...st Top	6A **30**	NG 876 651
...st Top	2D **47**	NC 210 273
...derton Hill	5A **92**	NH 719 824
...derton Sands	4B **92**	NH 732 846
...ean a' Chadh-fi	1D **53**	NC 213 510
...ean a' Chaoil	3A **26**	NG 812 563
...ean a' Ghamhna	5D **51**	NC 205 333
...ean a' Mhadaidh	2C **52**	NC 196 496
...ean an Achaidh	1F **49**	NC 121 338
...ean an Aigcioh	3A **52**	NC 153 488
...ean an Daraich	4D **11**	NH 438 590
...eanan Dubha	1C **52**	NC 188 518
...ean an Eireannaich	2D **53**	NC 202 503
...ean an Inbhire Bhàin		
	5F **25**	NG 793 550
...ean an t-Sabhail	5C **32**	NG 801 732
...ean an t-Sithein	1B **52**	NC 174 511
...ean Àrd	2C **52**	NC 185 503
...ean Bàgh	5A **50**	NC 140 322
...ean Choraidh	3C **58**	NC 421 580
...ean Chrona	1C **48**	NC 068 338
...ean Clùimhrig	4F **57**	NC 461 659
...ean Cnapach	4D **27**	NG 867 553
...ean Dornaidh Oscair		
	1A **50**	NC 157 406
...ean Dubh	1A **50**	NC 154 400
...ean Dubh	3A **52**	NC 159 489
...ean Dubh	3B **56**	NC 374 689
...ean Dubh	2D **59**	NC 435 610
...ean Dubh an Teoir	2C **52**	NC 193 494
...ean Dubh Chal Cinn		
	1F **49**	NC 120 336
...ean Dubh Dhrombaig		
	1F **49**	NC 122 334
...ean Dubh na		
Fionndalach Bige		
	2D **53**	NC 203 490
...ean Dubh nam Boc		
	2D **53**	NC 209 497
...ean Dubh na Sròine		
	2B **30**	NG 909 720
...ean Dùghaill	5F **25**	NG 794 546
...ean Eachainn	3D **31**	NG 932 718
...ean Eiglei	3C **64**	ND 780 658
...ean Garbh	5E **41**	NH 173 881
...ean Garbh	1A **50**	NC 145 404
...ean Glas	2A **52**	NC 156 491
...ean Hoan	3E **57**	NC 441 672
...ean Horrisdale	5B **32**	NG 786 744
...ean Loisgte	2C **30**	NG 912 730
...ean Meall a' Chaorainn		
	3E **53**	NC 220 485
...ean Mhic an Fhùlaraich		
	3D **31**	NG 937 713
...ean Mòr	3D **25**	NG 756 584
...ean Mòr	5B **98**	NH 503 568
...ean na Bearachd	2A **50**	NC 146 398
...ean na Creige Giubhais		
	3C **30**	NG 929 713
...ean na Gartaig	4C **44**	NC 218 124
...ean nan Caorach	1A **56**	NC 351 715
...ean nan Clachairean		
	3C **30**	NG 916 719
...ean nan Gall	1F **61**	NC 601 630
...ean nan Ròn	1B **62**	NC 639 655
...ean na Rainich	2A **50**	NC 142 394
...ean na Rainich	4E **51**	NC 228 343
...ean Port a' Choit	3D **53**	NC 214 480
...ean Rairidh	2C **50**	NC 164 351
...ean Riabhach	1A **50**	NC 146 407
...ean Ruairidh Beag	2B **30**	NG 896 728
...ean Ruairidh Mòr	2B **30**	NG 897 733
...ean Shieldaig	6C **32**	NG 803 729
...ean Sùbhainn	2C **30**	NG 923 721
...ean Thunga	4E **61**	NC 574 587
...drable Hill	3A **86**	NC 987 166
...nbo	6D **91**	NH 813 929
...nbo Muir	6C **90**	NH 798 919
...nbo Rocks	6D **91**	NH 818 920
...nbo Street	6C **90**	NH 799 913
...ag	3B **76**	ND 347 644
...glishton Muir	4C **6**	NH 610 440
...anton	4A **96**	NH 606 660
...anton Wood	4A **96**	NH 595 666
Faebait Wood	2B **8**	NH 493 511
Faire nam Fiadh	1A **12**	NH 250 669
Faraid Head	1B **56**	NC 389 715
Farley Wood	5B **8**	NH 492 469
Far North Top	3B **20**	NG 786 432
Farrmheall	3C **54**	NC 308 588
Farr Point	2F **63**	NC 716 645
Fas na Cleithe	5C **48**	NC 071 243
Fas Skerry	4D **79**	ND 385 513
Feadan	5C **48**	NC 071 248
Fearnmore	2C **24**	NG 724 606
Ferry View	3F **73**	ND 318 728
Ferry Wood	3D **91**	NH 814 971
Fionn Bheinn	1B **14**	NH 147 621
Firhill	2C **96**	NH 645 696
Flowerdale Forest	5A **30**	NG 887 673
Fodderty	3B **98**	NH 513 594
Foindle	3C **52**	NC 189 485
Forse Castle	3C **82**	ND 219 338
Forsie Moss	6D **69**	ND 048 625
Forss Water	5E **69**	ND 054 642
Four Parks	4B **90**	NH 776 956
Fourpenny	5C **90**	NH 801 940
Fourpenny Plantation	5C **90**	NH 796 931
Fraoch-eilean	5B **32**	NG 798 738
Fraoch Eilean Mòr	2D **35**	NG 948 911
Fresgoe	4F **67**	NC 957 659
Freswick Bay	1D **77**	ND 384 673
Fuar Tholl	1E **19**	NG 975 489
Gaineamh Mhòr	4C **32**	NG 804 757
Gairbh	3B **10**	NH 395 613
Gairbh Beag	2B **10**	NH 392 627
Gairloch	3B **32**	NG 796 775
Gairloch Caravan Park		
	3B **32**	NG 798 777
Gairloch Golf Club	4C **32**	NG 805 753
Gairloch Heritage Museum		
	4C **32**	NG 802 769
Gairloch Marine Life Centre		
& Cruises	3B **32**	NG 799 773
Gale Centre	3C **32**	NG 803 773
Gallow Hill	1B **6**	NH 597 501
Gallow Hill	5D **93**	NH 780 825
Gallow Hill	1E **93**	NH 802 902
Gallowhill Wood	2C **6**	NH 600 497
Gallows Hill	4D **99**	NH 543 589
Gallrope Bank	4D **93**	NH 789 851
Gansclet	2C **80**	ND 329 449
Garbh-Chnoc Mòr	6C **60**	NC 542 543
Garbh-eilean	1E **65**	NC 826 698
Garbh Chnoc	6E **61**	NC 570 539
Garbh Eilean	2C **30**	NG 913 724
Garbh Eilean	5E **51**	NC 224 339
Garbh Eilean	3E **53**	NC 224 474
Garbh Shron	6A **54**	NC 257 534
Garrie Island	5D **99**	NH 544 561
Garve	3B **10**	NH 395 613
Gaultiquoy	4B **78**	ND 346 505
Ghlas-Bheinn	2E **55**	NC 332 614
Giar Hill	5B **74**	ND 363 705
Gill, The	5F **71**	ND 201 675
Gills Bay	4A **74**	ND 331 733
Girnigoe Castle	2D **79**	ND 378 548
Gizzen Briggs	3F **93**	NH 817 876
Glac a' Chrotha	2C **10**	NH 312 566
Glac Àirigh an t-Saoir	5F **33**	NG 862 735
Glac a' Mhuchaidh	2E **15**	NH 214 615
Glac a' Mhuilinn	4E **39**	NH 190 798
Glac an Dunain	1F **33**	NG 864 829
Glac an Fheadair	6A **52**	NC 154 428
Glac an Fhuarain Ruaidh		
	3E **33**	NG 855 789
Glac an t-Seilich	1C **40**	NH 144 960
Glac an Tioraidh	4E **59**	NC 458 576
Glac Bhan	3C **38**	NH 169 810
Glac Bhàn	2C **10**	NH 416 630
Glac Bhàn	3F **13**	NH 353 629
Glac Bhàn	5A **32**	NG 769 746
Glac Bhàn a' Bhòcaidh		
	1A **32**	NG 770 820
Glac Bheithe	3B **40**	NH 113 921
Glac Bhreac	1A **14**	NH 125 628
Glac Bhuidhe	6E **27**	NG 885 517
Glac Bhuidhe	5A **32**	NG 766 744
Glac Bhuidhe	2F **35**	NH 988 917
Glac Bhuidhe	1C **40**	NH 141 977
Glac Chaol	5B **42**	NH 127 999
Glac Chaol	1A **96**	NH 602 713
Glac Cùilce	1D **49**	NC 093 330
Glac Dharach	6A **34**	NG 880 820
Glac Dhonn	6D **49**	NC 089 233
Glac Dhorch	6A **28**	NG 924 553
Glac Dhorch Bheag	4F **27**	NG 904 542
Glac Dhorch Mhòr	5F **27**	NG 902 539
Glac Dubh	4F **27**	NG 901 540
Glac Dubh a' Chaise	4E **27**	NG 897 540
Glac Dubh	2C **84**	ND 098 277
Glac Feàrna	1E **43**	NC 189 084
Glac Fionnar	5B **42**	NH 133 999
Glac Gharbh	2C **36**	NH 039 929
Glac Gheal	6A **32**	NG 764 710
Glac Iain Duibh	2D **31**	NG 944 730
Glack of Kessock	2E **7**	NH 655 484
Glac Luachrach	2C **10**	NH 414 638
Glac Luachrach	2A **36**	NG 996 923
Glac Luachrach	6F **51**	NC 240 301
Glac Mhàiri	3D **11**	NH 435 612
Glac Mhaolagain	6B **44**	NC 202 097
Glac Mhic Ruairidh	2B **36**	NH 020 915
Glac Mhòr	3B **34**	NG 897 898
Glac Mhòr	5B **52**	NC 179 447
Glac Mhòr	1A **96**	NH 609 719
Glac Mhòr a' Chòirn daraich		
	1F **15**	NH 224 628
Glac Mhòr an Fhas-uillt		
	2E **19**	NG 975 473
Glac Mhurchaidh	5F **33**	NG 866 734
Glac na Bò Chaisean	4D **27**	NG 879 543
Glac na Caillich	3E **13**	NH 337 633
Glac na Craoibhe Caorruinn		
	2A **44**	NC 186 175
Glac na Croiche	2C **40**	NH 135 943
Glac na Goibhre	4D **49**	NC 082 264
Glac na h-Airbhe	1D **39**	NH 172 850
Glac na h-Imrich	5D **49**	NC 087 256
Glac nam Bac	6E **27**	NG 882 505
Glac nan Capull	5A **34**	NG 871 852
Glac nan Each	6C **14**	NH 177 539
Glac nan Each	5D **27**	NG 876 520
Glac nan Each	4A **36**	NH 008 878
Glac nan Each	2D **39**	NH 171 843
Glac nan Làrach Liatha		
	5B **42**	NC 132 007
Glac na Sròine	3C **36**	NH 034 903
Glac Scap	3D **41**	NH 152 938
Glac Sheilich	2F **35**	NG 987 903
Glac Shìldeig	6C **32**	NG 804 721
Glac Sleibhe	5B **32**	NG 786 743
Glac Tric	1E **23**	NG 729 539
Glas-eilean Mòr	2E **65**	NC 820 689
Glas Bheinn	3B **18**	NG 902 440
Glas Bheinn	2F **47**	NC 254 264
Glas Chnoc	1B **46**	NC 171 286
Glas Leac	1C **52**	NC 180 518
Glas Mheall Liath	6E **37**	NH 077 841
Glas Mheall Mòr	5E **37**	NH 076 853
Gleann a' Bhaile Dheirg		
	5C **32**	NG 812 743
Gleann a' Ghrobain	5D **33**	NG 836 745
Gleann Airigh Chomhaich		
	4C **30**	NG 928 693
Gleannan a' Choit	2B **46**	NC 165 270
Gleannan an Fheadair	5C **48**	NC 060 256
Gleannan Bad na Bàighe		
	4D **53**	NC 215 462
Gleannan nan Caorach		
	6D **51**	NC 217 318
Gleannan Salach	3F **49**	NC 137 284
Gleannan Salach	6D **49**	NC 086 235
Gleann Ardbhair	5C **50**	NC 180 332
Gleann Chaorachain	2A **38**	NH 110 844
Gleann Creagach	5D **67**	NG 919 634
Gleann Crom	4A **34**	NG 873 861
Gleann Dorcha	2B **44**	NC 191 176
Gleann Leireag	6B **50**	NC 168 304
Gleann Marcasaidh	6F **13**	NH 356 578
Gleann Mòr	5E **39**	NH 190 785
Gleann na Sguaib	2F **39**	NH 223 841
Gleann na Speireig	1B **98**	NH 503 648
Gleann Scourie	5B **52**	NC 176 441
Gleann Sgathaich	3E **11**	NH 457 609
Gleann Tùlacha	2F **31**	NG 987 738
Glebe	4F **7**	NH 664 457
Glen Aldie	1C **94**	NH 756 793
Glenarigolach	3F **35**	NG 982 894
Glencanisp Forest	5A **46**	NC 155 199
Glen Carron	4C **16**	NH 059 504
Glencarron and		
Glenuig Forest	4F **17**	NH 111 492
Glengolly	6A **70**	ND 101 658
Glen Grudie	1B **28**	NG 957 655
Glen Kerry	5C **32**	NG 817 735
Glen Loth	2E **15**	NC 945 106
Glen of Foulis	1E **99**	NH 573 632
Glen of Scotsburn	2A **94**	NH 722 781
Glen Shieldaig	6B **26**	NG 835 503

Glen Torridon .... 6A 28 NG 931 563
Golden Valley .... 5A 16 NH 012 471
Golspie .... 2E 91 NC 835 003
Golspie Golf Club .... 3D 91 NH 822 986
Golval Hill .... 6C 66 NC 908 613
Gorm Chnoc .... 1A 46 NC 150 287
Gorm Chnoc .... 5D 53 NC 218 447
Gorstan .... 2B 10 NH 389 622
Gower .... 4B 98 NH 507 582
Grannie's Heilan'
  Hame Holiday
  Park .... 6D 91 NH 818 924
Green Hillock............. 4F 93 NH 821 842
Grottistoft Moss .... 4D 73 ND 272 704
Grudie .... 3D 13 NH 308 620
Gruinard Bay Caravan Park
  .... 2B 34 NG 901 918

H.M. Prison Inverness
  .... 4F 7 NH 668 448
Halladale Inn Caravan
  & Chalet Park .... 4B 66 NC 888 642
Halladale River .... 6C 66 NC 894 611
Harriet Plantation ...... 5A 90 NH 765 931
Harril Head................ 4C 80 ND 312 392
Hartmount .... 2C 94 NH 760 776
Haster .... 4A 78 ND 325 511
Haugh .... 4F 7 NH 666 446
Head of Crees............. 2F 73 ND 319 743
Heathmount Wood .... 1C 94 NH 761 793
Hebridean Whale Cruises
  .... 4C 32 NG 806 751
Heights of Brae........... 2C 98 NH 521 613
Helmsdale Golf Club..... 3C 86 ND 024 160
Helmsdale Rock........... 3C 86 ND 029 165
Helmsdale Youth Hostel
  .... 3C 86 ND 029 154
Henrietta Park .... 4E 97 NH 687 656
Highfield Park............. 1E 9 NH 551 530
Highland Wildcat Trails
  .... 1E 91 NC 839 014
Hillhead .... 2E 83 NC 257 355
Hill of Achalone .... 6D 69 ND 031 630
Hill of Buolglass .... 3A 82 ND 170 322
Hill of Clais-na-canaich
  .... 5A 80 ND 270 386
Hill of Clayton............ 3B 76 ND 342 636
Hill of Clindrag .... 5E 71 ND 170 673
Hill of Crogodale........ 5D 75 ND 397 713
Hill of Fearn .... 2F 95 NH 827 783
Hill of Forss
  or Scrabster Hill
  .... 3F 69 ND 070 690
Hill of Foulis .... 1E 99 NH 579 644
Hill of Harland .... 3A 78 ND 325 537
Hill of Harley .... 2D 77 ND 375 659
Hill of Leodebest......... 2B 82 ND 184 350
Hill of Longstone .... 4B 80 ND 300 397
Hill of Lybster............ 3C 68 ND 023 693
Hill of Lychrobbie .... 3A 82 ND 170 322
Hill of Mid Clyth.......... 5A 80 ND 285 385
Hill of Nigg................ 6F 95 NH 820 705
Hill of Oliclett .... 1B 80 ND 292 461
Hill of Olrig................ 6E 71 ND 174 656
Hill of Quintfall .... 4A 76 ND 314 624
Hill of Rattar.............. 2B 72 ND 246 731
Hill of Rigifa' .... 3E 73 ND 304 721
Hill of Rive .... 3F 71 ND 198 722
Hill of Shebster........... 5C 68 ND 012 645
Hill of Slickly.............. 5E 73 ND 299 681
Hill of Stemster........... 4B 78 ND 342 504
Hill of Stroupster .... 2B 76 ND 337 660
Hill of Tain .... 6B 92 NH 739 811
Hill of Toftcarl .... 6C 78 ND 355 461
Hill of Toftgunn .... 3A 80 ND 270 423
Hill of Ulbster .... 3D 81 ND 331 422
Hill of Warse .... 5A 74 ND 337 716
Hill of Wester .... 6A 76 ND 319 579
Hill of Whitefield .... 6F 71 ND 198 659
Hill of Yarrows .... 3B 80 ND 296 427
Hill o' Many Stanes,
  Mid Clyth .... 5B 80 ND 290 384
Hilton .... 5F 7 NH 673 434
Hilton .... 6C 90 NH 804 916
Hilton .... 6E 93 NH 795 800
Historylinks Museum .. 2E 93 NH 795 895
Holborn Head.............. 3A 70 ND 107 715
Holborn Hill............... 3A 70 ND 095 712
Holborn Head Lighthouse
  .... 4A 70 ND 106 707
Holburndmey Moss ...... 4D 73 ND 283 705
Hope .... 2F 59 NC 474 601
Hunting Hill............... 6E 93 NH 808 803

Inbhir Nis.................. 4F 7 NH 666 454
Inchberry Hill............. 4B 6 NH 598 446
Incheril .... 3F 29 NH 034 620
Inchgarve Forest......... 4E 35 NG 964 875
Inchmore................... 4A 6 NH 569 449
Inchnadamph .... 5F 47 NC 251 216
Inner Sound............... 3B 74 ND 353 748
Inshegra .... 5A 54 NC 250 549
Inver .... 4A 82 ND 169 301
Inveralligin .... 3C 26 NG 843 574
Inver Caravan Park, Dunbeath
  .... 4A 82 ND 166 303
Inverewe Gardens .... 1E 33 NG 858 820
Inverewe Gardens Caravan
  & Camping Club Site
  .... 2F 33 NG 861 809
Invergordon .... 3F 97 NH 707 685
Invergordon Golf Club
  .... 2F 97 NH 693 693
Inver Hill .... 5D 85 ND 112 217
Inverness .... 4F 7 NH 666 454
Inverness Botanic Gardens
  .... 5E 7 NH 657 436
Inverness Caledonian Thistle F.C.
  .... 3F 7 NH 673 470
Inverness Golf Club...... 4F 7 NH 679 443
Inverness Millburn
  Youth Hostel .... 4F 7 NH 663 444
Inverness Museum
  & Art Gallery .... 4F 7 NH 666 443
Island of Stroma.......... 2B 74 ND 353 773
Isle Maree .... 2D 31 NG 931 723

James Pringle Weavers
  of Inverness .... 5E 7 NH 655 430
Jamestown .... 5F 11 NH 476 565
Janetstown .... 5F 69 ND 084 653
John o' Groats............ 4C 74 ND 383 726
John o' Groats
  Caravan Site .... 4C 74 ND 383 731
John o' Groats
  Youth Hostel .... 4B 74 ND 350 720

Keiss .... 4B 76 ND 345 615
Kenmore .... 4D 25 NG 757 573
Keoldale.................... 5C 46 NC 382 660
Kerry Wood .... 5C 32 NG 818 741
Kildary .... 3C 94 NH 768 750
Kildary Wood .... 4C 94 NH 753 740
Killin Rock .... 4A 88 NC 868 058
Kilmuir .... 4C 94 NH 756 731
Kinlochewe .... 3F 29 NH 029 619
Kinmylies.................. 4E 7 NH 648 443
Kirkhill..................... 5E 9 NH 553 454
Kirkton .... 5B 18 NG 913 412
Kirkton .... 3C 90 NH 798 985
Kirtomy .... 4A 64 NC 742 635
Kirtomy Point .... 3A 64 NC 749 657
Kishorn .... 4D 21 NG 830 403
Kishorn Island .... 6C 20 NG 806 376
Knockan .... 5C 44 NC 213 105
Knockan Crag National
  Nature Reserve .... 6B 44 NC 199 098
Knockbain.................. 6E 9 NH 552 432
Knockbreck................ 6D 93 NH 786 811
Knockfarrel................ 4B 98 NH 507 580
Knock Farril .... 4B 98 NH 505 585
Knocknagael Boar Stone
  .... 6E 7 NH 658 409
Knock Rash................ 4A 96 NH 599 661
Kyle of Durness .... 1F 55 NC 368 637
Kyle of Tongue .... 3E 61 NC 586 595
Kylesku..................... 5E 51 NC 228 335
Kylestrome .... 4E 51 NC 220 344

Ladiesloch .... 5B 88 NC 899 044
Lady Flat .... 2A 96 NH 600 701
Lael Forest .... 1E 39 NH 201 852
Laide .... 2B 34 NG 900 919
Laidhay Croft Museum
  .... 1F 85 ND 157 304
Lamigo .... 2C 62 NC 653 632
Lamington .... 3B 94 NH 740 764
Landhallow .... 3B 82 ND 187 336
Langwell Plantation ..... 5C 84 ND 107 226
Latheron .... 3B 82 ND 198 335
Latheronwheel............ 3B 82 ND 185 329
Leabaidh Aonghais Chonnoich
  .... 2F 63 NC 719 646
Leac Bhuidhe .... 6A 34 NG 872 839
Leac Mhòr .... 3C 66 NC 898 660

Leacnasaide .... 6B 32 NG 796 7
Leac na Saighde .... 5B 32 NG 798 7
Leathad Buidhe........... 2D 29 NG 993 6
Leathad Mòr............... 4A 34 NG 878 8
Leckmelm.................. 4D 41 NH 165 9
Leckmelm Forest......... 4E 41 NH 189 9
Leckmelm Wood.......... 4D 41 NH 163 9
Ledgowan Forest......... 1F 17 NH 101 5
Lednagullin .... 4D 65 NC 801 6
Leirinbeg .... 3D 57 NC 416 6
Leirinmore .... 4D 57 NC 420 6
Lemlair..................... 2E 99 NH 571 6
Lentran..................... 4B 6 NH 582 4
Leth Chreag .... 3F 31 NG 979 7
Letterewe Forest......... 2F 31 NG 976 7
Letters...................... 6D 41 NH 162 8
Liathach .... 3F 27 NG 913 5
Lieurary.................... 6E 69 ND 069 6
Littleferry................. 4C 90 NH 805 9
Little Garve .... 2B 10 NH 392 6
Little Loch Broom .... 3B 40 NH 015 9
Little Scatwell............ 5B 10 NH 387 5
Little Wyvis .... 1D 11 NH 429 6
Loandhu .... 2F 95 NH 815 7
Loch a' Bhaid-luachraich
  .... 4B 34 NG 896 8
Loch a' Chàirn Bhàin ... 5D 51 NC 201 3
Loch Achall .... 2E 41 NH 177 9
Loch a' Chroisg .... 3A 14 NH 130 5
Loch A' Mhuilinn NNR
  .... 2B 50 NC 161 3
Loch an Inbhir............ 6D 49 NC 089 2
Lochardil .... 5F 7 NH 661 4
Loch Assynt............... 4E 47 NC 228 2
Loch Baligill Hill......... 5A 66 NC 857 6
Loch Broom................ 2B 40 NH 113 9
Lochcarron .... 6A 18 NG 894 3
Lochcarron Golf Club
  .... 5B 18 NG 915 4
Loch Damh................. 6D 27 NG 865 5
Loch Diabaig.............. 3F 25 NG 790 5
Loch Dùghaill .... 1C 52 NC 186 5
Lochend.................... 5C 72 ND 265 6
Loch Eriboll............... 4F 57 NC 468 6
Loch Eriboll Lighthouse
  .... 2E 59 NC 457 6
Loch Eye................... 1F 95 NH 829 7
Loch Fleet .... 4B 90 NH 780 9
Loch Fleet National
  Nature Reserve .... 4B 90 NH 781 9
Loch Garve .... 4C 10 NH 410 5
Loch Glencoul .... 6F 51 NC 257 3
Loch Hope .... 5E 59 NC 462 5
Loch Inver .... 6C 48 NC 067 2
Lochinver.................. 6D 49 NC 089 2
Loch Kanaird .... 5A 42 NH 106 9
Loch Kishorn.............. 5D 21 NG 825 3
Loch Laxford.............. 2C 52 NC 188 5
Loch Luichart .... 3E 13 NH 335 6
Loch Lurgainn .... 1B 42 NC 123 0
Loch Maree................ 2B 30 NG 906 7
Loch Maree Islands
  National Nature
  Reserve
  .... 3C 30 NG 922 7
Loch na h-Oidhche...... 6A 30 NG 889 6
Lochrosque Forest........ 1B 14 NH 154 6
Lochshell .... 3C 78 ND 353 5
Loch Shieldaig............ 4A 26 NG 801 5
Loch Torridon .... 2E 25 NG 760 6
Loch Urigill .... 6D 45 NC 244 0
Loch Veyatie .... 4B 44 NC 196 1
Logie Hill .... 3C 94 NH 766 7
Lonbain.................... 1C 22 NG 686 5
Lonemore .... 3B 32 NG 786 7
Lonemore .... 2C 92 NH 767 8
Long Wood................. 5D 9 NH 533 4
Lord Berkeley's Seat .... 6D 37 NH 064 8
Lothbeg .... 2E 15 NC 945 1
Lothmore................... 5A 86 NC 960 1
Lotts .... 3C 62 NC 669 6
Lower Badcall............. 1B 50 NC 165 4
Lower Brora .... 5C 88 NC 903 0
Lower Clashmore Plantation
  .... 2C 92 NH 755 8
Lower Diabaig .... 2F 25 NG 794 6
Lower Drummond........ 5F 7 NH 664 4
Lower Tullich .... 5B 94 NH 742 7
Luichart Power Station
  .... 3D 13 NH 312 6
Lybster .... 2E 83 ND 247 3
Lybster Golf Club......... 3D 51 ND 250 3
Lythe Berry .... 4E 71 NH 177 6
Lythmore Moss .... 4E 69 ND 063 6

ac is Màthair .... 4D 37 NH 068 876
ainreachan Buttress... 1E 19 NG 971 488
aoile nan Gamhnach
.... 6A 12 NH 248 578
aol Chalaisgeig .... 2D 41 NH 150 942
aol Chean-Dearg ...... 1C 18 NG 924 499
aol na Bruaich .... 4A 34 NG 883 875
aovally Beag .... 1C 54 NC 308 637
aovally More............. 1D 55 NC 317 636
arrel .... 2C 86 ND 019 170
arybank .... 1B 8 NH 480 535
arybank Wood .... 3C 94 NH 752 765
aryburgh .... 5D 99 NH 540 565
as na Buaile............. 2D 63 NC 672 635
avesy........................ 1F 83 ND 260 361
eabhaich .... 4B 66 NC 879 647
eall a' Bhainne .... 3B 38 NH 140 814
eall a' Bhainne .... 6E 39 NH 190 755
eall Achadh Deisteil ... 4C 32 NG 811 761
eall a' Chairn .... 1C 38 NII 150 857
eall a' Chaorainn ...... 2A 14 NH 136 604
eall a' Choire Bhuidhe
.... 4A 26 NG 819 546
eall a' Choire Ghlais... 1D 31 NG 931 752
eall a' Choire Lèith .. 6E 13 NH 325 573
eall a' Chuaille .... 4E 43 NC 191 027
eall a' Chuilinn .... 2B 44 NH 300 622
eall a' Chuna Mòr ..... 4D 49 NC 085 269
eall a' Cliuth .... 2E 33 NG 850 800
eall a' Ghiuthais .... 2C 28 NG 976 634
eall a' Ghuail............ 1B 98 NH 512 643
eall a' Giubhas .... 3E 29 NH 005 614
eall Àirigh Mhic Criadh
.... 3D 33 NG 831 773
eall a' Mhuthaich...... 2B 44 NC 191 172
eallan a' Mhùthaidh Beag
.... 2D 13 NH 310 647
eallan a' Mhùthaidh Mòr
.... 1D 13 NH 312 661
eallan an Lochain-Ghiubhais
.... 3C 34 NG 912 890
eallan Buidhe............ 3C 12 NH 280 635
eall an Buidhe .... 5A 42 NC 111 000
eall an Daimh .... 2C 18 NG 924 470
eallan Dìomhain .... 5A 44 NC 170 116
eall an Doire .... 1F 33 NG 861 825
eall an Doireachain ... 3E 23 NG 732 491
eallan Doire Bheithe
.... 3A 16 NH 010 510
eall an Doirein .... 4E 33 NG 858 754
eall an Duibhe........... 1B 38 NH 133 859
eall an Eich Ghlais.... 1F 41 NH 208 970
eall an Fheadain .... 2B 58 NC 391 611
eall an Fhithich .... 1F 59 NG 994 456
eall an Fhliuchaird .... 4D 17 NH 067 495
eallan Ghobhar .... 2F 29 NH 029 645
eallan Gobhar .... 1E 21 NG 844 465
eall an Leathaid Dharaich
.... 1F 33 NG 878 810
eall an Leathaid Mhòir
.... 2A 16 NH 001 546
eallan Liath Mòr........ 1C 44 NC 222 186
eall an Lochain Ruaidh
.... 3B 62 NC 635 614
eallan Mhic Aonghais
.... 4D 33 NG 839 765
eallan Mhic Iamhair... 2D 17 NH 068 542
eallan Mhurchaidh..... 1C 44 NC 214 188
eallan na Circe-Fraoich
.... 4E 29 NH 008 605
eallan Odhar .... 1E 15 NH 208 631
eall an Spardain .... 4E 33 NG 854 758
eall an t-Siomlair....... 5F 25 NC 781 554
eall an t-Sithe .... 6B 38 NH 141 765
eallan Udrigill .... 1B 34 NG 893 929
eall an Ulbhaidh .... 2D 50 NC 214 497
eall Arachaidh .... 3F 23 NG 749 498
eall Aundrary .... 3B 32 NG 846 728
eall Bad a' Chròtha ... 6A 32 NG 772 725
eall Bad a' Mhartuin .. 4D 59 NC 442 564
eall Bad a' Mhuidhe... 5D 59 NC 439 557
eall Bhad Ghaineamhaich
.... 6D 13 NH 318 576
eall Breac .... 6F 39 NH 223 750
eall Buidhe .... 3D 35 NG 937 892
eall Ceann na Creige
.... 2A 26 NG 804 595
eall Chnàimhean ...... 1C 30 NG 920 758
eall Coire an Lochain
.... 2F 43 NC 211 065
eall Cruaidh .... 4F 41 NH 202 912
eall Dearg................. 5D 25 NG 754 546
eall Dearg................. 3F 27 NG 913 579
eall Dearg................. 1C 42 NC 148 087

Meall Dearg................. 1B 54 NC 273 620
Meall Deise .... 2D 33 NG 875 875
Meall Dhonuill .... 2C 84 ND 107 273
Meall Doire Fàid......... 4F 39 NH 220 792
Meall Dubh .... 2C 38 NH 166 838
Meall Dubh na Drochaid
.... 6E 27 NG 899 504
Meall Fearna.............. 3E 29 NH 010 618
Meall Fuaraidh .... 4D 33 NG 832 758
Meall Gaineamhach... 3C 22 NG 693 490
Meall Garbh .... 5D 37 NH 062 865
Meall Garbh .... 1A 40 NH 098 976
Meall Garbhaig .... 4B 30 NG 906 691
Meall Glac Àirigh an t-Saoir
.... 5F 33 NG 864 739
Meall Glac na Daraich... 2A 32 NG 760 808
Meall Glac Tigh-fàil .... 3C 38 NH 161 828
Meall Glas.................. 1A 62 NG 629 659
Meall Gorm .... 4A 20 NG 779 409
Meall Gorm .... 5D 27 NG 874 522
Meall Imireach........... 1B 32 NG 791 821
Meall Leathad na Craoibhe
.... 6A 62 NC 615 557
Meall Lochan a' Chleirich
.... 3A 30 NG 872 716
Meall Loch an Fheòir.... 5E 23 NG 732 440
Meall Loch an Fhìdhleir
.... 3C 24 NG 729 586
Meall Lochan na Geala
.... 4A 30 NG 887 680
Meall Loch nan Gamhna
.... 5B 62 NC 646 581
Meall Meadhonach.......3A 54 NC 268 581
Meall Meadhonach.......6D 57 NC 410 627
Meall Mhèinnidh .... 1E 31 NG 954 748
Meall Mhic Iomhair.....1D 13 NH 316 673
Meall Mòr .... 6A 18 NG 898 391
Meall Mòr .... 2B 32 NG 796 808
Meall Mòr .... 1A 40 NH 102 974
Meall Mòr .... 5B 42 NC 137 002
Meall Mòr .... 3F 61 NC 605 603
Meall na Braclaich....... 2B 44 NC 193 160
Meall na Caorach .... 3C 84 ND 099 269
Meall na Coille .... 4D 25 NG 748 572
Meall na Doire Gairbhe
.... 6B 34 NG 898 826
Meall na Dubh Chlaise
.... 3B 32 NG 798 788
Meall na Fhuaid .... 2E 23 NG 738 502
Meall na h-Àirde .... 6D 21 NG 821 373
Meall na h-Àirde .... 4A 32 NG 769 742
Meall na h-Airighe Riabhaich
.... 1A 34 NG 872 932
Meall na h-Araid .... 3F 25 NG 788 588
Meall nam Bacan .... 3A 30 NG 883 713
Meall na Mèine .... 4A 30 NG 880 698
Meall na Mòine........... 4C 54 NC 293 567
Meall na Mòine........... 1B 54 NC 283 620
Meall nan Ceapairean .. 1C 18 NG 937 486
Meall nan Clach Ruadha
.... 5F 61 NC 605 569
Meall nan Crà .... 3A 58 NC 378 590
Meall nan Dearcag Mòr
.... 2F 43 NC 200 065
Meall nan Doireachan... 5F 39 NH 229 784
Meall nan Garbh Loch
.... 2D 49 NC 082 304
Meall nan Uan .... 6B 34 NG 902 832
Meall na Teanga Fhiadhaich
.... 2D 19 NG 941 469
Meall Odhar .... 1E 43 NC 197 078
Meall Preas a' Chreamha
.... 1F 43 NC 212 080
Meall Riabhach .... 1E 29 NH 010 666
Meall Ruighe an Fhirich
.... 2C 10 NH 414 620
Meall Sùil a' Chròtha .... 5A 34 NG 880 852
Meall Thailm .... 1A 62 NG 629 662
Meann Chnoc .... 3A 96 NH 597 684
Melvich...................... 4B 66 NC 879 647
Melwich Bay.............. 4B 66 NC 888 655
Merkinch .... 3F 7   NH 660 460
Mey Hill .... 2F 73 ND 312 740
Mial........................... 3B 32 NG 797 780
Mid Hill ....1A 86 NC 982 209
Midtown..................... 3E 61 NC 580 609
Millbank.................... 5B 70 ND 118 678
Millburn..................... 4F 7   NH 676 455
Mill Hill..................... 3B 94 NH 749 758
Milnafua .... 2E 97 NH 674 701
Milton........................ 2A 6   NH 579 495
Milton........................ 4B 78 ND 349 509
Milton........................ 4C 94 NH 763 741
Milton Moss .... 6A 68 NC 984 621

Miltown .... 6D 23 NG 707 438
Modsary.................... 3C 62 NC 650 618
Moine Bhog .... 6C 34 NG 924 835
Mòine Mhòr .... 1C 16 NH 056 557
Mòine Mhòr .... 1F 21 NG 865 462
Mol Mòr .... 4E 27 NG 894 556
Mool Hill .... 4B 74 ND 365 726
Morangie Forest .... 6B 92 NH 733 814
Morefield .... 2B 40 NH 113 958
Moruisg..................... 4F 17 NH 101 499
Mossford Power Station
.... 3E 13 NH 330 631
Moss of Brough......... 2A 72 ND 217 734
Moss of Burracks ...... 4A 94 NH 720 740
Moss of Dunnet......... 2F 71 ND 209 739
Moss of Forse .... 1D 83 ND 220 363
Moss of Greenland.... 6B 72 ND 249 656
Moss of Iresgoe .... 1E 81 ND 352 451
Moss of Quintfall ...... 4A 76 ND 318 623
Moss of Tain............. 6B 72 ND 235 654
Moss of Wcstcr......... 6A 76 ND 311 589
Moss of West Mey..... 3D 73 ND 276 721
Moss of Whilk .... 4B 80 ND 292 406
Mound Rock .... 3B 90 NH 779 988
Mountain And Sea Guides
.... 5D 23 NG 712 443
Mountgerald.............. 2E 99 NH 567 615
Mountpleasant........... 5B 70 ND 125 682
Mountvernon.............. 5B 70 ND 114 674
Moy Island .... 1B 8   NH 487 545
Moy Wood .... 5A 98 NH 492 557
Muckernich Wood....... 6F 99 NH 595 537
Muireachies, The ...... 4C 70 ND 144 701
Muir of Allangrange .... 2E 9   NH 557 527
Muir of Ord .... 3D 9   NH 528 501
Muir of Ord Golf Club... 3D 9   NH 528 491
Mullach a' Bheithe ..... 6D 33 NG 826 723
Mullach an Àird .... 4B 64 NC 752 647
Mullach an Rathain ...... 3F 27 NG 911 576
Mullach na Creige Deirge
.... 3B 52 NC 168 473
Murkle....................... 5D 71 ND 164 679
Murray's Plantation..... 1D 93 NH 775 908

Na Rathanan .... 1D 27 NG 873 613
Naver Rock .... 4E 63 NC 701 590
Neave Island or Coomb Island
.... 2C 62 NC 664 644
Nedd......................... 2F 49 NC 136 319
Ness Islands .... 5F 7   NH 661 435
Ness of Portnaculter ... 4B 92 NH 741 848
New Craig.................. 3D 81 NH 341 418
Newhall..................... 4F 97 NH 691 653
Newlands of Geise .... 6A 70 ND 090 658
Newmills.................... 5E 97 NH 680 649
Newmore .... 2E 9   NH 550 522
Newport..................... 4D 85 ND 125 239
Newton Hill .... 5C 78 ND 350 490
Newton Moss .... 5B 78 ND 344 494
Nigg........................... 5E 95 NH 804 716
Nigg Bay.................... 6C 94 NH 768 709
North Brora Muir .... 5B 88 NC 884 040
North Coast Visitor Centre
.... 5B 70 ND 112 683
Northern Pinnacles ...... 3F 27 NG 913 579
Northfield.................... 1F 97 NH 703 718
North Kessock .... 3E 7   NH 655 478
North Killimster .... 2A 78 ND 326 554
North Strathconon Forest
.... 4F 15 NH 233 566
North Top .... 3B 20 NH 785 424
North West Highlands
Geopark Visitor Centre
.... 5E 51 NC 236 320
Noss Head .... 2D 79 ND 387 548
Noss Head Lighthouse
.... 2D 79 ND 388 549
Nybster...................... 3C 76 ND 359 634

Oak Dell..................... 1C 8   NH 516 542
Ord Hill .... 2F 7   NH 664 491
Ormlie .... 5A 70 ND 107 677
Osties Hill .... 4C 80 ND 316 408
Overton .... 6A 80 ND 288 365

Pàirc Mhòr................. 3C 40 NH 145 936
Pairc na Froise .... 3D 19 NG 952 444
Papigoe .... 4D 79 ND 381 515
Pennyland .... 5A 70 ND 107 684
Pilkington's Gully .... 6A 46 NC 148 184
Pitcalnie.................... 5E 95 NH 805 723

Pitmaduthy Moss......... 2D **95** NH 779 776
Points of Tang............ 4C **70** ND 138 700
Poles................... 6B **90** NH 782 929
Poll na Caorach.......... 2B **92** NH 732 882
Poolewe.................. 2E **33** NG 858 807
Portgower................ 4B **86** ND 005 133
Portskerra............... 4B **66** NC 875 657
Portvasgo or Port Vasgo
.... 1E **61** NC 583 648
Preas Mòr............... 2F **55** NC 356 603
Pump Room.............. 4A **98** NH 482 573

Quinag.................. 1D **47** NC 204 293

Rabbit Islands .... 1F **61** NC 601 630
Rae Berry................ 4E **71** ND 174 693
Rattar Moss.............. 3D **73** ND 271 729
Raven Rock.............. 3F **11** NH 463 604
Raven's Hill.............. 3E **69** ND 068 691
Reay.................... 5A **68** NC 973 649
Reay Golf Club.......... 4F **67** NC 966 650
Redcastle................ 2B **6** NH 582 495
Red Moss................ 4A **80** ND 281 401
Red Moss................ 1B **82** ND 191 376
Red Point................ 4E **67** NC 930 658
Redstone Hill............ 3F **71** ND 199 727
Reidhleacach............ 6C **20** NG 817 367
Reismeave............... 3C **64** NC 787 653
Reiss................... 2B **78** ND 331 543
Resolis.................. 4D **97** NH 668 652
Rheindown............... 4C **8** NH 519 476
Rheindown Wood .... 4C **8** NH 504 477
Rhiconich .... 1F **53** NC 256 524
Rhiroy.................. 4D **41** NH 151 900
Rhitongue............... 3F **61** NC 600 592
Rhue................... 1A **40** NH 099 971
River Beauly............. 4E **9** NH 551 478
River Bran............... 4A **12** NH 254 612
River Bran............... 3D **15** NH 197 594
River Brora.............. 5A **88** NC 868 046
River Carron............. 6A **14** NH 121 538
River Carron............. 5B **16** NH 028 489
River Carron............. 3E **17** NH 097 528
River Carron............. 5C **18** NG 928 409
River Carron............. 3E **19** NG 977 452
River Conon .... 1C **8** NH 508 539
River Conon .... 5B **10** NH 387 578
River Conon .... 6C **98** NH 539 556
River Dionard .... 3E **55** NC 332 579
River Dionard .... 5B **56** NC 374 643
River Evelix.............. 2C **92** NH 752 887
River Fleet............... 2A **90** NH 760 993
River Helmsdale .... 2B **86** ND 000 179
River Meig............... 6A **10** NH 366 559
River Meig............... 5F **17** NH 117 479
River Naver.............. 5F **63** NC 711 579
River Orrin.............. 2A **8** NH 466 517
Riverside Caravan
Club Site .... 4C **78** ND 353 511
Riverside Chalets
& Caravan Park....... 6E **11** NH 457 555
River Strathy............. 5E **65** NC 827 621
River Thurso............. 6B **70** ND 110 654
Rosebank Plantation ..... 2F **15** NH 235 615
Rose Hill................ 1B **94** NH 746 798
Ross County Football Club
.... 4D **99** NH 555 587
Rough of Stain........... 5B **76** ND 345 602
Round Hill............... 6A **72** ND 229 652
Royal Dornoch Golf Club
.... 2E **93** NH 798 889
Ruadh-Stac Beag .... 3C **28** NG 972 613
Ruadh-Stac Mòr .... 3B **28** NG 951 611
Ruadh Stac Bheag .... 2C **18** NG 921 475
Rubha a' Bhacain........ 6C **48** NC 060 227
Rubha a' Bhuirdeasaich
.... 6D **49** NC 080 223
Rubha a' Ghiuthais...... 3B **26** NG 824 571
Rubha Àird Choinnich
.... 2B **24** NG 709 606
Rubha an Aird Bhig...... 3C **64** NC 776 659
Rubha an Fhir Lèith...... 5D **51** NC 208 330
Rubha an Ròin .... 4A **26** NG 800 543
Rubha an Tuir .... 4C **66** NC 895 656
Rubh a' Bhad Choill ..... 1A **50** NC 154 412
Rubha Bhrà.............. 3B **66** NC 876 665
Rubha Blar Bog .... 5D **41** NH 164 899
Rubha Buidhe............ 2C **24** NG 731 601
Rubha Cadail .... 1A **40** NH 093 974
Rubha Chuaig........... 3A **24** NG 699 589
Rubha Creag Iomhair... 1E **49** NC 103 337
Rubha Dubh.............. 2C **62** NC 657 638

Rubha Fitheachaig .... 1B **48** NC 052 325
Rubha Geal.............. 2B **62** NC 645 637
Rubha Ghoiridh .... 3B **66** NC 873 664
Rubha Gisgil............. 1B **50** NC 165 405
Rubha Giuthais.......... 5A **42** NH 101 996
Rubha Glas.............. 3D **25** NG 751 584
Rubh' Aird an t-Sionnaich
.... 5A **52** NC 144 434
Rubha Leumair........... 4B **48** NC 043 262
Rubha Meallain Bhuidhe
.... 5A **42** NH 113 997
Rubha Meil Cuilce........ 2E **65** NC 815 686
Rubha Mhic Chonnuill
.... 5B **32** NG 791 736
Rubh' a' Mhill Dheirg ... 3A **48** NC 029 285
Rubh' a' Mhucard........ 2B **50** NC 161 380
Rubh' a' Mhuilt.......... 1F **59** NC 474 624
Rubha na Bà............. 3D **53** NC 208 485
Rubha na Fèarna........ 2C **24** NG 721 612
Rubha na Feòla.......... 4C **26** NG 842 551
Rubha na Griosaich...... 4E **57** NC 440 659
Rubha na Guailne .... 5C **22** NG 690 457
Rubha na h-Àirde Bige
.... 2D **53** NC 209 502
Rubha na Maoile......... 4A **50** NC 145 343
Rubha nam Meallan ..... 3B **64** NC 765 663
Rubha na Mòine .... 3C **24** NG 738 599
Rubha nan Eanntag...... 5C **32** NG 806 737
Rubh' an Daimh.......... 4E **57** NC 446 655
Rubha Ruadh............ 1B **52** NC 164 511
Rubha Shiòs............. 5A **52** NC 140 448
Rubh' Dhubhard .... 1F **49** NC 132 335
Ruigh Dorch............. 6B **50** NC 161 309
Ruighe-Chnoc .... 4F **45** NC 287 124
Ruighean an Aitinn...... 1F **49** NC 127 329
Ruighean Thòmais ...... 5C **50** NC 197 330
Ruigh Mheallain......... 4C **36** NH 033 872
Ruith Chnoc............. 4E **43** NC 197 020
Russian Arctic Convoy
Museum .... 3A **34** NG 877 893
Ruttle Wood .... 6B **8** NH 483 438

Sàil Bheag.............. 3B **36** NH 018 900
Sàil Gharbh .... 1D **47** NC 209 292
Sàil Ghorm.............. 6C **50** NC 198 304
Sàil Mhòr .... 4A **28** NG 938 605
Sàil Mhòr .... 4C **36** NH 033 887
Sàil na Cloiche Mòire ... 1F **23** NG 740 525
St Andrew's Cathedral,
Inverness .... 4F **7** NH 662 448
St Duthus's Chapel,
Tain .... 5D **93** NH 785 822
St John's Point......... 1F **73** ND 310 751
St Mary's Chapel,
Crosskirk .... 2C **68** ND 024 700
St Peter's Church,
Thurso............... 5B **70** ND 118 684
Saltburn................ 6A **94** NH 722 695
Sand Hills .... 4D **65** NC 793 643
Sands of Nigg .... 5D **95** NH 784 721
Sangobeg .... 4D **57** NC 426 663
Scaniport............... 6D **7** NH 631 400
Scaraben .... 3A **84** ND 066 268
Scarf Rocks .... 3F **67** NC 958 662
Scarfskerry .... 2D **73** ND 276 745
Scorguie .... 3E **7** NH 647 461
Scotsburn Wood .... 3A **94** NH 726 769
Scourie .... 5A **52** NC 154 446
Scourie Caravan
& Camping Park ..... 5A **52** NC 152 445
Scourie Mor .... 5A **52** NC 152 439
Scrabster............... 4A **70** ND 098 700
Seadrift Visitor Centre
.... 3A **72** ND 212 712
Seana Mheallan .... 6A **28** NG 928 551
Seaview Farm Caravan Park
.... 6C **90** NH 806 913
Second Coast .... 2C **34** NG 928 906
Serpent Hillock .... 5D **71** ND 160 682
Sgeir a' Bhuic.......... 1F **59** NC 471 630
Sgeir a' Ghair .... 2C **24** NG 724 615
Sgeir an Fheòir .... 6C **20** NG 810 364
Sgeir an Òir .... 2A **62** NC 611 643
Sgeir an Trilleachain.... 1A **50** NC 155 402
Sgeir Chreagach .... 6B **18** NG 906 388
Sgeireán Mòra.......... 5F **25** NG 795 549
Sgeir Fhada .... 6B **18** NG 912 395
Sgeir Iosal .... 2B **52** NC 178 507
Sgeir na Tràghad ...... 4A **48** NC 035 276
Sgeir Ruadh .... 3B **66** NC 881 660
Sgeir Uistein .... 1A **50** NC 157 413
Sgòrr a' Chadail .... 3E **27** NG 893 579
Sgòrr Deas............. 2A **42** NC 102 068

Sgòrr Tuath.............. 1A **42** NC 110 07
Sgòrr a' Chaorachain.... 4B **40** NC 796 4
Sgurrachd Ire........... 5F **13** NH 341 5
Sgùrr a' Choire-rainich
.... 6A **12** NH 247 5
Sgùrr a' Gharaidh ...... 3A **18** NG 884 4
Sgùrr a' Gharraidh ..... 4C **16** NH 040 4
Sgùrr a' Ghlas Leathaid
.... 6A **12** NH 243 5
Sgùrr Bàn .... 4C **28** NG 974 6
Sgùrr Creag an Eich .... 6D **37** NH 055 8
Sgùrr Dubh .... 6C **28** NG 979 5
Sgùrr Dubh .... 2F **31** NG 988 7
Sgùrr Fiòna .... 6D **37** NH 064 8
Sgùrr Marcasaidh ...... 5F **13** NH 353 5
Sgùrr Mòr.............. 1D **27** NG 865 6
Sgùrr na Bana-Mhoraire
.... 5D **27** NG 870 5
Sgùrr na Feartaig .... 6C **16** NH 055 4
Sgùrr nan Ceannaichean
.... 5E **17** NH 087 4
Sgùrr nan Conobhan ... 4A **20** NG 762 4
Sgùrr nan Fhir Duibhe
.... 4D **29** NG 981 6
Sgùrr Ruadh .... 5C **36** NH 040 8
Shearwater Cruises ..... 3B **40** NH 128 9
Sheepy Hillock.......... 2F **73** ND 313 7
Shieldaig .... 5A **26** NG 816 5
Shieldaig Camping and Cabins
.... 6A **18** NG 819 5
Shieldaig Island .... 4A **26** NG 810 5
Shillinghill.............. 2D **97** NH 658 6
Shore Caravan Site ..... 5B **48** NC 052 2
Sibster................. 3A **78** ND 326 5
Sidheanan Dubha........ 2A **32** NG 770 7
Sidhean an Loch-chlàir
.... 6A **32** NG 778 7
Sidhean Ard .... 6B **50** NC 168 3
Sidhean Mòr .... 1C **14** NH 173 6
Sidhean Mòr Cnoc Thormaid
.... 6C **52** NC 191 4
Sìdhean na Cloiche Muilinn
.... 5A **50** NC 158 3
Sie Skerry .... 3F **73** ND 328 7
Sildeag .... 5A **26** NG 816 5
Sinclair Castle .... 2D **79** ND 381 5
Sinclair's Bay .... 6C **76** ND 360 5
Sinclair's Bay
including Ackergill...... 1C **78** ND 357 5
Sithean a' Mhill......... 1F **25** NG 784 6
Sithean Mòr .... 6C **32** NG 811 7
Sithean Mòr .... 5D **33** NG 836 7
Sithean Mòr .... 1F **55** NC 360 6
Sithean na Gearrsaich
.... 6F **61** NC 605 5
Sithean na h-Àirde ..... 5A **32** NG 777 7
Sithean na Sròine ...... 5E **39** NH 195 7
Skelbo .... 4C **90** NH 790 9
Skelbo Castle .... 4C **90** NH 791 9
Skelbo Wood .... 5B **90** NH 781 9
Skerhardies .... 4C **76** ND 356 6
Skerray .... 2B **62** NC 643 6
Skinnet .... 2E **61** NC 588 6
Skirza, Skirza Harbour
& Freshwick Bay ..... 1E **77** ND 390 6
Slates, The............. 4B **70** ND 125 6
Slattadale Forest .... 2A **30** NG 881 7
Sloping Head............ 2F **69** ND 072 7
Slumbay Island......... 6A **18** NG 895 3
Smithstown............. 3B **32** NG 793 7
Smoo.................. 3D **57** NC 415 6
Smoo Cave .... 3D **57** NC 419 6
Socach Hill............. 4B **88** NC 884 06
Sound of Handa......... 3A **52** NC 153 48
South Kessock .... 3E **7** NH 657 46
Soyea Island .... 6B **48** NC 048 22
Spear Head .... 3A **70** ND 096 7
Spears, The............. 2E **69** ND 063 7
Speicein Còinnich ...... 3A **42** NC 107 04
Spidean a' Choire Lèith
.... 5A **28** NG 929 5
Spidean Còinich........ 2D **47** NC 206 27
Spidean Coire nan Clach
.... 4C **28** NG 966 59
Spidean Toll nam Biast
.... 6E **27** NG 887 5C
Spital Wood .... 1A **6** NH 560 5C
Springpark .... 5B **70** ND 122 67
Spur, The............... 4E **71** ND 170 69
Srath a' Bhàthaich...... 1A **18** NG 892 48
Srath a' Chrom-Uillt .... 6E **45** NC 251 08
Srathan Buidhe .... 1D **31** NG 943 74
Srath Beag .... 6A **58** NC 386 53
Srath Cùil.............. 4C **84** ND 103 23

ath Dionard............ 5D **55** NC 324 557
ath Fèith an Leòthaid
.... 5D **47** NC 201 211
ath Gairbh............... 3C **10** NH 403 616
ath Lungard............ 6C **30** NG 919 648
ath Maolchaluim....... 3F **23** NG 740 481
ath Mòr .... 1C **40** NH 143 969
ath na Bèiste........... 3A **36** NH 000 899
ath Nimhe............... 4F **41** NH 201 905
òn a' Bhuic............. 4B **46** NC 170 220
òn a' Choire............ 5D **37** NH 065 851
òn a' Choit .... 3B **30** NG 904 705
òn a' Chròchair........ 3D **87** ND 041 155
òn a' Mahàis .... 4F **25** NG 781 577
òn Creag na Ceapaich
.... 3E **37** NH 078 899
òndubh.................. 1F **33** NG 862 813
an Gharbh.............. 3A **84** ND 054 266
ac an Fhlithich......... 5B **48** NC 054 244
axigoe .... 3D **79** ND 383 523
ob a' Choire Liath Mhòr
.... 5A **28** NG 932 581
ber .... 3B **48** NC 041 298
or......................... 3B **48** NC 041 298
rath .... 3B **32** NG 797 774
rath Beag .... 4F **37** NH 099 874
rath Bran .... 2F **15** NH 231 608
rathbran Forest........ 3B **12** NH 266 634
rathbran Plantation ... 2E **15** NH 210 611
rath Canaird .... 4C **42** NC 158 021
rathcanaird............. 4C **42** NC 150 018
rath Carron .... 3E **19** NG 976 454
rathcarron Brewery ... 4D **19** NG 947 420
rathdrynie .... 3C **98** NH 539 602
rath Garve.............. 3B **10** NH 396 619
rathgarve Forest ...... 1C **10** NH 416 648
rath Lunndaidh........ 2B **90** NC 787 007
rath Melness .... 1D **61** NC 565 640
rath Mòr .... 5A **50** NC 146 330
rath More................ 3D **39** NH 189 820
rathnasheallag Forest
.... 6C **36** NH 041 843
rathnaver Museum .... 3F **63** NC 714 622
rathnaver Trail .... 5F **63** NC 722 575
rath of Baillie .... 6F **69** ND 050 652
rath Peffer.............. 3B **98** NH 510 595
rathpeffer............... 4A **98** NH 483 581
rathpeffer Spa Golf Club
.... 4F **11** NH 479 584
rathpeffer Youth Hostel
.... 4A **98** NH 480 570
rath Sgitheach .... 1C **98** NH 529 634
rath Tongue .... 4A **62** NC 620 591
rathtongue .... 4A **62** NC 619 594
rathy .... 3F **65** NC 839 653
rathy .... 4A **84** ND 067 241
rathy Bay .... 3F **65** NC 838 661
rathy Point .... 2E **65** NC 821 674
rathy Point Lighthouse
.... 1E **65** NC 827 695
roma Lighthouse ...... 1B **74** ND 353 792
rone Nea................ 2E **39** NH 194 844
rone Wood.............. 5E **39** NH 193 785
roupster Forest......... 6F **73** ND 322 658
uc a' Choire Dhuibh Bhig
.... 5B **28** NG 942 582
uc Coire an Laoigh.... 4C **28** NG 966 592
uc Loch na Cabhaig
.... 1E **27** NG 891 616

Swiney .... 2D **83** ND 237 355
Swiney Hill.............. 2D **83** ND 239 343
Swordly .... 4A **64** NC 733 630
SW Top .... 1B **38** NH 148 855
Sydera Wood .... 2C **92** NH 769 890

Tain....................... 5D **93** NH 780 820
Taindore Pasture ...... 2C **6** NH 614 497
Taindore Wood........... 1F **7** NH 676 509
Tain Golf Club .... 5E **93** NH 796 823
Talmine .... 2E **61** NC 585 625
Tang Head .... 5C **76** ND 353 608
Tansfield .... 5F **71** ND 196 671
Tarbat Mains .... 4C **94** NH 764 735
Tarbet.................... 3B **52** NC 165 487
Tarlogie Wood......... 5C **92** NH 758 825
Tarvie Wood............ 4E **11** NH 441 582
Teandalloch............. 4C **8** NH 518 485
Thistly Hill............... 1D **77** ND 375 676
Thrumster................ 1C **80** ND 328 450
Thurso................... 5B **70** ND 116 684
Thurso Art Gallery........ 5B **70** ND 115 681
Thurso Bay .... 4B **70** ND 116 699
Thurso East............. 5B **70** ND 123 686
Thurso East
    & Thurso Harbour.. 4B **70** ND 122 694
Thurso Golf Club .... 6A **70** ND 096 664
Tighnafiline .... 3A **34** NG 870 894
Timespan Museum
    and Arts Centre...... 3C **86** ND 025 153
Tofts .... 6B **74** ND 368 685
Toll a' Meitheach .... 5A **28** NG 939 574
Tom Apigill .... 6E **63** NC 707 568
Tomich................... 2F **97** NH 700 709
Tom na Caillich......... 1D **11** NH 438 653
Tom na Gruagaich ... 1C **26** NG 859 601
Tongue .... 5F **61** NC 591 567
Tongue Bay .... 2F **61** NC 607 617
Tongue Wood............ 3F **61** NC 597 592
Tongue Youth Hostel.... 4E **61** NC 587 585
Tordale Park............. 4E **69** ND 068 665
Torgormack............. 6B **8** NH 485 449
Torlogie Scalps......... 4B **92** NH 746 851
Tòrr a' Bhealaidh ...... 4B **8** NH 495 486
Tòrr a' Bhealaidh ...... 4A **8** NH 471 484
Tòrr a' Bhealaidh ...... 5A **10** NH 367 567
Torr Achilty............. 6E **11** NH 447 550
Torrachilty Forest....... 6D **11** NH 437 557
Torrachilty Wood........ 6D **11** NH 430 557
Tòrr an Làir.............. 6C **10** NH 418 558
Torran na Baintighearna
.... 4B **8** NH 491 475
Tòrr an Uinnein .... 6D **11** NH 420 556
Torr Breac............... 2C **10** NH 401 633
Torr Dubh .... 2C **84** ND 101 281
Torridon .... 4F **27** NG 905 557
Torridon .... 4F **27** NG 902 558
Torridon Campsite ...... 3F **27** NG 906 561
Torridon Countryside Centre
.... 4E **27** NG 899 554
Torridon Forest......... 2D **27** NG 870 594
Torridon Youth Hostel
.... 3F **27** NG 902 562
Torrisdale .... 3D **63** NC 677 616
Torrisdale Bay .... 3D **63** NC 689 625
Tòrr Mòr................ 6B **8** NH 486 436
Tòrr Mòr................ 2E **35** NG 956 913
Tòrr na Bithe .... 2E **59** NC 453 605

Torvean Golf Club .... 5E **7** NH 646 438
Totegan .... 2E **65** NC 828 677
Tothel Gill Forest .... 1B **76** ND 345 674
Tournaig .... 6A **34** NG 876 835
Tower Wood .... 2A **8** NH 476 520
Town House, Dingwall
.... 4D **99** NH 551 589
Tràigh Allt Chàilgeag .... 4E **57** NC 442 656
Tubeg .... 2C **62** NC 659 635
Tullich Wood .... 4A **94** NH 729 743
Tulloch Hill.............. 2C **98** NH 538 620
Turriegoe Hill .... 3D **81** ND 346 426

Ullapool .... 2B **40** NH 129 942
Ullapool Golf Club .... 2B **40** NH 122 949
Ullapool Point........... 3B **40** NH 125 938
Ullapool Youth Hostel... 2B **40** NH 129 940
Unapool.................. 5E **51** NC 236 329
Uppat Wood .... 6B **88** NC 881 024
Upper Badcall.......... 6A **52** NC 156 421
Upper Drummond ...... 5F **7** NH 668 436
Upper Loch Torridon ... 3C **26** NG 850 561
Urchany and Farley Forest
.... 4A **8** NH 467 473
Urray..................... 2C **8** NH 509 524
Ussie Wood .... 5B **98** NH 512 567

Viaduct Plantation ..... 4B **12** NH 271 618
Victoria Falls .... 3B **30** NG 895 707

Warehouse Hill .... 3B **80** ND 308 411
Warse.................... 5A **74** ND 334 718
Warth Hill .... 6C **74** ND 371 698
Watch Hill, The......... 4A **62** NC 611 594
WDCS Dolphin
    and Seal Centre ..... 2E **7** NH 654 482
Wee Campsite, The ..... 5A **18** NG 899 401
West Clyne.............. 4B **88** NC 889 058
Wester Alligin.......... 2B **26** NG 831 580
Wester Balblair .... 5C **8** NH 509 451
Wester Brae............ 6D **97** NH 652 619
Wester Lonvine .... 5A **94** NH 713 728
Westfield .... 5E **69** ND 058 641
Westford................. 2C **96** NH 645 693
West Helmsdale........ 3C **86** ND 020 154
West Raeberry .... 4C **70** ND 148 702
West Strathan .... 1D **61** NC 566 644
Weydale Moss .... 6C **70** ND 135 656
Weydale Strand .... 4E **71** ND 183 691
Whale's Back........... 2D **69** ND 037 714
Whaligoe .... 4C **80** ND 318 407
Whin Island............. 5E **7** NH 657 433
Whiteface................ 2A **92** NH 711 888
Wick...................... 4C **78** ND 363 510
Wick Golf Club .... 1B **78** ND 339 562
Wick Heritage Museum
.... 4C **78** ND 366 505
Wilderness, The......... 3B **94** NH 735 756
Willowbank............. 4C **78** ND 368 510
Windhill.................. 4D **9** NH 530 480
Woodside of Tollie ..... 5B **98** NH 515 566

Yarrows Archaeological Trail
.... 2B **80** ND 306 433
Yellow Moss .... 5C **68** ND 020 647

North Coast 500 - Route Planner

Inverness to Inverness

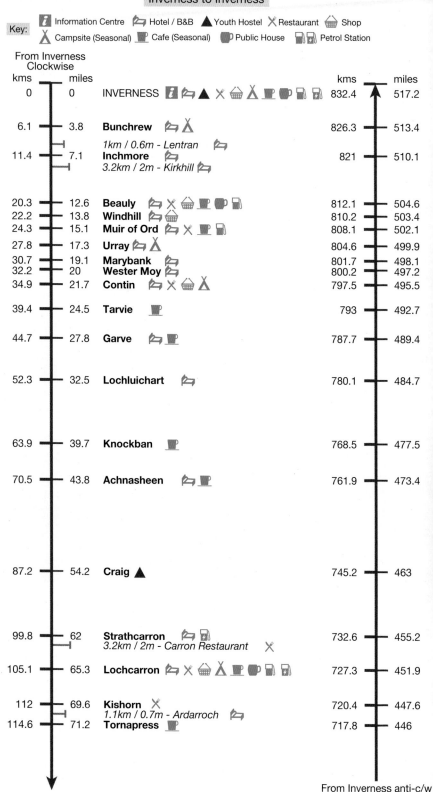

Key: Information Centre · Hotel / B&B · Youth Hostel · Restaurant · Shop · Campsite (Seasonal) · Cafe (Seasonal) · Public House · Petrol Station

From Inverness Clockwise

kms	miles		kms	miles
0	0	INVERNESS	832.4	517.2
6.1	3.8	**Bunchrew**	826.3	513.4
		1km / 0.6m - Lentran		
11.4	7.1	**Inchmore**	821	510.1
		3.2km / 2m - Kirkhill		
20.3	12.6	**Beauly**	812.1	504.6
22.2	13.8	**Windhill**	810.2	503.4
24.3	15.1	**Muir of Ord**	808.1	502.1
27.8	17.3	**Urray**	804.6	499.9
30.7	19.1	**Marybank**	801.7	498.1
32.2	20	**Wester Moy**	800.2	497.2
34.9	21.7	**Contin**	797.5	495.5
39.4	24.5	**Tarvie**	793	492.7
44.7	27.8	**Garve**	787.7	489.4
52.3	32.5	**Lochluichart**	780.1	484.7
63.9	39.7	**Knockban**	768.5	477.5
70.5	43.8	**Achnasheen**	761.9	473.4
87.2	54.2	**Craig**	745.2	463
99.8	62	**Strathcarron**	732.6	455.2
		3.2km / 2m - Carron Restaurant		
105.1	65.3	**Lochcarron**	727.3	451.9
112	69.6	**Kishorn**	720.4	447.6
		1.1km / 0.7m - Ardarroch		
114.6	71.2	**Tornapress**	717.8	446

From Inverness anti-c/w

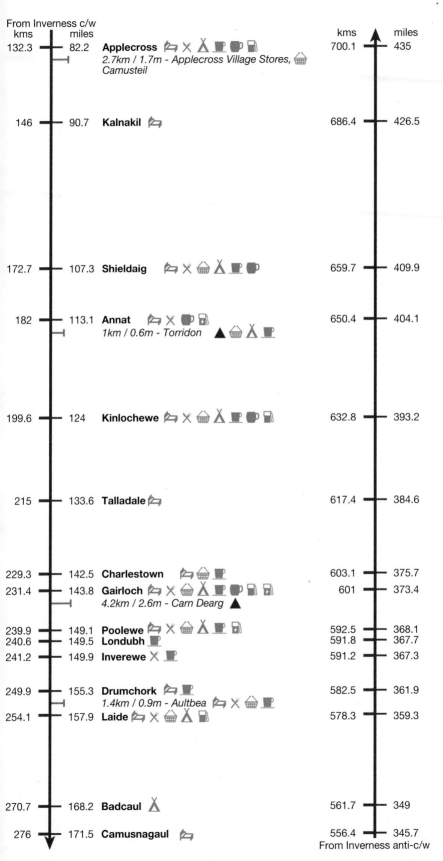

From Inverness c/w				
kms	miles		kms	miles

kms	miles		kms	miles
132.3	82.2	**Applecross**	700.1	435
		2.7km / 1.7m - Applecross Village Stores,		
		Camusteil		
146	90.7	**Kalnakil**	686.4	426.5
172.7	107.3	**Shieldaig**	659.7	409.9
182	113.1	**Annat**	650.4	404.1
		1km / 0.6m - Torridon		
199.6	124	**Kinlochewe**	632.8	393.2
215	133.6	**Talladale**	617.4	384.6
229.3	142.5	**Charlestown**	603.1	375.7
231.4	143.8	**Gairloch**	601	373.4
		4.2km / 2.6m - Carn Dearg		
239.9	149.1	**Poolewe**	592.5	368.1
240.6	149.5	**Londubh**	591.8	367.7
241.2	149.9	**Inverewe**	591.2	367.3
249.9	155.3	**Drumchork**	582.5	361.9
		1.4km / 0.9m - Aultbea		
254.1	157.9	**Laide**	578.3	359.3
270.7	168.2	**Badcaul**	561.7	349
276	171.5	**Camusnagaul**	556.4	345.7

From Inverness anti-c/w

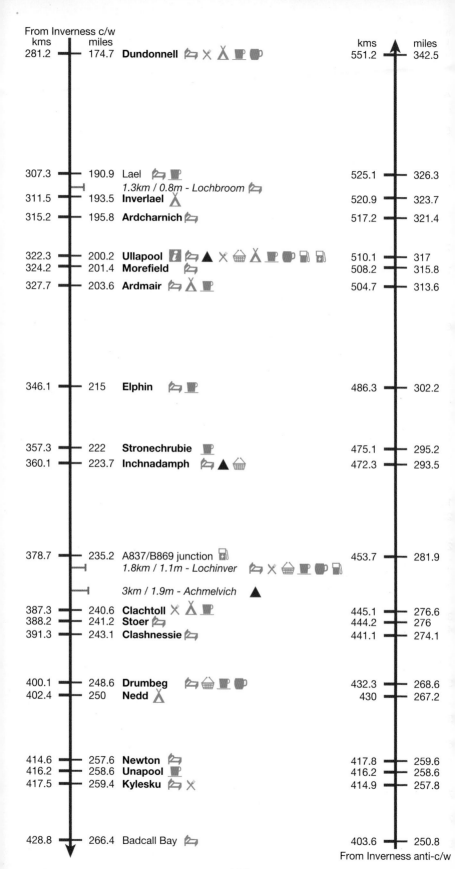

From Inverness c/w			
kms	miles		
281.2	174.7	**Dundonnell**	551.2 · 342.5

From Inverness c/w
kms · miles

281.2 — 174.7 **Dundonnell**
551.2 — 342.5

307.3 — 190.9 Lael
525.1 — 326.3
1.3km / 0.8m - Lochbroom
311.5 — 193.5 **Inverlael**
520.9 — 323.7
315.2 — 195.8 **Ardcharnich**
517.2 — 321.4

322.3 — 200.2 **Ullapool**
510.1 — 317
324.2 — 201.4 **Morefield**
508.2 — 315.8
327.7 — 203.6 **Ardmair**
504.7 — 313.6

346.1 — 215 **Elphin**
486.3 — 302.2

357.3 — 222 **Stronechrubie**
475.1 — 295.2
360.1 — 223.7 **Inchnadamph**
472.3 — 293.5

378.7 — 235.2 A837/B869 junction
453.7 — 281.9
1.8km / 1.1m - Lochinver

3km / 1.9m - Achmelvich

387.3 — 240.6 **Clachtoll**
445.1 — 276.6
388.2 — 241.2 **Stoer**
444.2 — 276
391.3 — 243.1 **Clashnessie**
441.1 — 274.1

400.1 — 248.6 **Drumbeg**
432.3 — 268.6
402.4 — 250 **Nedd**
430 — 267.2

414.6 — 257.6 **Newton**
417.8 — 259.6
416.2 — 258.6 **Unapool**
416.2 — 258.6
417.5 — 259.4 **Kylesku**
414.9 — 257.8

428.8 — 266.4 Badcall Bay
403.6 — 250.8

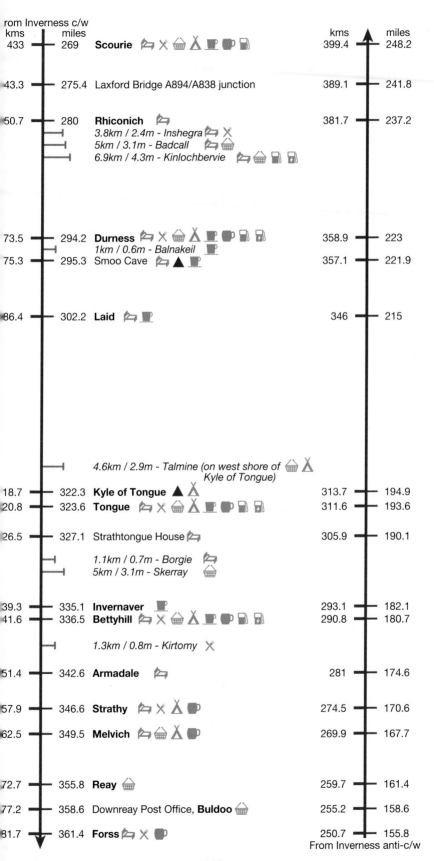

From Inverness c/w

kms	miles		kms	miles
433	269	**Scourie** 🛏️ ✕ 🧺 ⛺ 🚰 ☕ ⛽	399.4	248.2
443.3	275.4	Laxford Bridge A894/A838 junction	389.1	241.8
450.7	280	**Rhiconich** 🛏️	381.7	237.2
		3.8km / 2.4m - Inshegra 🛏️ ✕		
		5km / 3.1m - Badcall 🛏️ 🧺		
		6.9km / 4.3m - Kinlochbervie 🛏️ 🧺 ⛽ ⚡		
473.5	294.2	**Durness** 🛏️ ✕ 🧺 ⛺ 🚰 ☕ ⛽	358.9	223
		1km / 0.6m - Balnakeil ☕		
475.3	295.3	Smoo Cave 🛏️ ▲ 🚰	357.1	221.9
486.4	302.2	**Laid** 🛏️ 🚰	346	215
		4.6km / 2.9m - Talmine (on west shore of 🧺 ⛺		
		Kyle of Tongue)		
518.7	322.3	**Kyle of Tongue** ▲ ⛺	313.7	194.9
520.8	323.6	**Tongue** 🛏️ ✕ 🧺 ⛺ 🚰 ☕ ⛽	311.6	193.6
526.5	327.1	Strathtongue House 🛏️	305.9	190.1
		1.1km / 0.7m - Borgie 🛏️		
		5km / 3.1m - Skerray 🧺		
539.3	335.1	**Invernaver** 🚰	293.1	182.1
541.6	336.5	**Bettyhill** 🛏️ ✕ 🧺 ⛺ 🚰 ☕ ⛽ ⚡	290.8	180.7
		1.3km / 0.8m - Kirtomy ✕		
551.4	342.6	**Armadale** 🛏️	281	174.6
557.9	346.6	**Strathy** 🛏️ ✕ ⛺ ☕	274.5	170.6
562.5	349.5	**Melvich** 🛏️ 🧺 ⛺ ☕	269.9	167.7
572.7	355.8	**Reay** 🧺	259.7	161.4
577.2	358.6	Downreay Post Office, **Buldoo** 🧺	255.2	158.6
581.7	361.4	**Forss** 🛏️ ✕ ☕	250.7	155.8

From Inverness anti-c/w

113

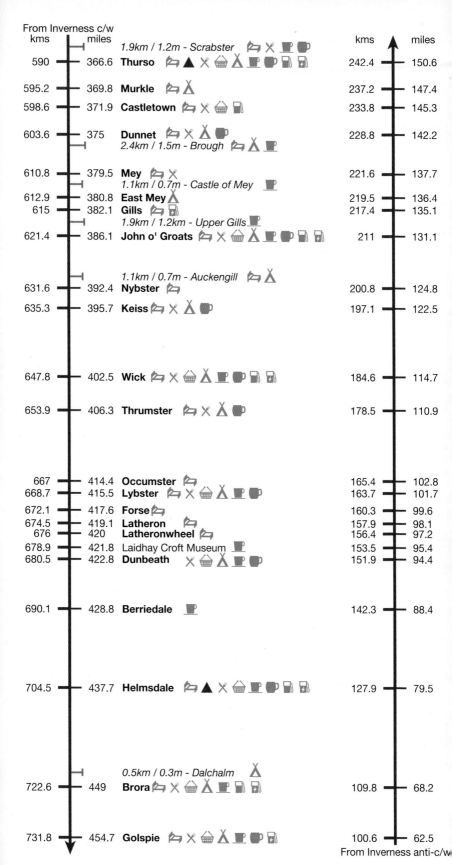

From Inverness c/w

kms	miles		kms	miles
		1.9km / 1.2m - Scrabster		
590	366.6	**Thurso**	242.4	150.6
595.2	369.8	**Murkle**	237.2	147.4
598.6	371.9	**Castletown**	233.8	145.3
603.6	375	**Dunnet**	228.8	142.2
		2.4km / 1.5m - Brough		
610.8	379.5	**Mey**	221.6	137.7
		1.1km / 0.7m - Castle of Mey		
612.9	380.8	**East Mey**	219.5	136.4
615	382.1	**Gills**	217.4	135.1
		1.9km / 1.2km - Upper Gills		
621.4	386.1	**John o' Groats**	211	131.1
		1.1km / 0.7m - Auckengill		
631.6	392.4	**Nybster**	200.8	124.8
635.3	395.7	**Keiss**	197.1	122.5
647.8	402.5	**Wick**	184.6	114.7
653.9	406.3	**Thrumster**	178.5	110.9
667	414.4	**Occumster**	165.4	102.8
668.7	415.5	**Lybster**	163.7	101.7
672.1	417.6	**Forse**	160.3	99.6
674.5	419.1	**Latheron**	157.9	98.1
676	420	**Latheronwheel**	156.4	97.2
678.9	421.8	Laidhay Croft Museum	153.5	95.4
680.5	422.8	**Dunbeath**	151.9	94.4
690.1	428.8	**Berriedale**	142.3	88.4
704.5	437.7	**Helmsdale**	127.9	79.5
		0.5km / 0.3m - Dalchalm		
722.6	449	**Brora**	109.8	68.2
731.8	454.7	**Golspie**	100.6	62.5

From Inverness anti-c/w

114

kms	miles		kms	miles
737.6	458.3	Beech Tree Lodge, **Loch Fleet**	94.8	58.9
740.3	460	Strathview Lodge, **Cambusavie**	92.1	57.2
744.7	462.7	**Poles**	87.7	54.5
		5.3km / 3.3m - Embo		
		3km / 1.9m - Dornoch		
747.4	464.4	**Evelix**	85	52.8
		0.2km / 0.1m - Clashmore		
755	469.1	Dornoch Firth (Meikle Ferry)	77.4	48.1
758.9	471.5	**Tain**	73.5	45.7
		9km / 5.6m - Nigg		
767.7	477	**Ballchraggan**	64.7	40.2
768.0	477.2	**Kildary**	64.4	40
768.5	477.5	**Milton**	63.9	39.7
772.5	480	**Delny**	59.9	37.2
776.2	482.3	**Tomich**	56.2	34.9
779.9	484.6	**Dalmore**	52.5	32.6
		1.4km / 0.9m - Alness		
784	487.1	Skiach Services	48.4	30.1
		1.4km / 0.9m - Evanton		
		3.2km / 2m - Mountgerald		
797.5	495.5	**Dingwall**	34.9	21.7
801	497.7	**Maryburgh**	31.4	19.5
802.3	498.5	**Conon Bridge**	30.1	18.7
808.1	502.1	**Muir of Ord**	24.3	15.1
810.2	503.4	**Windhill**	22.2	13.8
812.1	504.6	**Beauly**	20.3	12.6
814.7	506.2	Beauly Holiday Park	17.7	11
		3.2km / 2m - Kirkhill		
821	510.1	**Inchmore**	11.4	7.1
		1km / 0.6m - Lentran		
826.3	514.4	**Bunchrew**	6.1	3.8
832.4	517.2	INVERNESS	0	0

From Inverness
Anti-clockwise

· Most campsites and caravan sites are seasonal and may not be open in the winter, check before going.
· Some caravan sites are for Caravan Club members only, check before going.
· Some cafes are open only in the summer.
· For more information on safely driving on the North Coast 500, campervans, camping, and leaving no trace
  go to pages 116 -118.

Tourist Information Centres

Name	Address	Telephone
Inverness	36 High Street, Inverness. IV1 1JQ	01463 252401
Ullapool	Argyle Street, Ullapool. IV26 2UB	01854 612486

Driving on the North Coast 500

The 516 miles of this wonderful touring route pass through the stunning scenery of the Northern Highlands, much of it around one of the most beautiful coastlines in the world. For the benefit of your own enjoyment of the route and that of fellow tourers, and out of polite consideration for local inhabitants drive patiently, courteously and responsibly.

General road safety

For the safety of all road users, it is important to read the road ahead and anticipate potential hazards.

- Take care approaching bends and be cautious at hairpin corners.
- Beware of hidden dips, blind summits and concealed entrances. Bear in mind that any of these could be hiding pedestrians, cyclists, slow-moving or broken-down vehicles, deer or sheep.
- Long stretches of road are unfenced so be watchful of grazing animals and pass with care.
- Do slow right down approaching more vulnerable road users such as horse riders, cyclists and pedestrians, and wait to pass at a point where you can give them as much room as another vehicle.
- Overgrown verges on country roads may impede visibility or conceal potential hazards.
- Always drive within the speed limit. In wet or icy conditions, reduce your speed so that you have a safe stopping distance.
- Be prepared for sudden changes in the weather and be mindful of flooded and slippery road surfaces, with boggy verges, after heavy rainfall.
- Do plan ahead before each leg of your journey, as there are often long distances between filling stations or public charging points.
- Allow for rest stops on your journey and breaks to enjoy the scenery.

Single track roads

Particular care is needed on single track roads. Know the Highway Code and the driving etiquette for their use, especially the protocol on passing places, which are usually marked by a white square or diamond sign:

- Stay on the left.
- Pull into a passing place to let oncoming traffic through.
- Do not impede traffic behind you and use a passing place to permit vehicles to overtake.
- If the passing place is on your right, wait opposite to allow traffic to pass.
- Do not travel in convoy as many passing places only have room for a single vehicle.
- Do not park in passing places.
- Be prepared to reverse on single track roads to allow oncoming traffic to pass.
- Do give a friendly thank you to other road users who have waited or pulled over.
- Brake before the peak of a blind summit.
- Slow down when you see animals on or beside the road.
- Do not block field access.
- Remember too that single track roads are vital for emergency services and deliveries to rural communities, and they are the only way to work, school, shops and other amenities for local people.

Driving a motorhome or campervan
If your motorhome is more than a standard VWT5 conversion (i.e. about 16–18 feet, or approx. 5 metres, in length), please take the alternative motorhome routes available. Please do not attempt to drive the Bealach na Bà (instead, take the A832) or B869 Drumbeg road (take the A894).

- If you cannot accurately reverse your vehicle several hundred yards on a narrow single track road, you cannot safely drive the NC500.
- Use passing places to allow any traffic that has built up behind you to overtake safely.
- Do not travel in convey. Always travel at least one passing place apart.

Overnight parking
Please make use of the designated motorhome and campervan sites along the NC500. These have the facilities you need to make your road trip comfortable and enjoyable, and in using them you help to support the local economy.
- Be aware that 'wild camping' is only permitted by those travelling on foot or using non-motorised transport. DO NOT wild camp in your campervan or motorhome.
- Never stay overnight in sites that specifically state 'No overnight camping'.
- At busy times of the year, campsites can get booked up and so if you are unable to secure a pitch, please see the NC500 website for alternative, informal motorhome stops: www.northcoast500.com
- Other helpful advice on touring in Scotland and overnight stops can be found on the CAMPA website (Campervan & Motorhome Professional Association): www.campa.org.uk

Daytime stops
Use common sense in regard to the vehicle you are travelling in and the location:
- Ensure the place you stop is suitable for your vehicle.
- Take great care to avoid damaging grassland and verges, and other sensitive wildlife habitat.
- Do not block gateways.
- Use parking bays appropriately and avoid overcrowding.
- Follow any on-site regulations regarding the use of BBQs or fires and do not leave evidence of these behind.
- Ensure your vehicle is self-contained with toilet facilities and waste water tanks, and that these are only emptied at campsites and other designated waste disposal points.
- Leave your stop-off space clean and tidy, taking litter with you and disposing of it responsibly.

Cycling on the North Coast 500
Touring by bike is a more adventurous way of travelling round the northern Highlands. It can be a fantastic experience, but please bear the following in mind.
- Don't expect motorists to see you. Be aware that the nature of country roads, with sharp bends, hidden dips, blind summits, concealed turnings and overgrown verges, and Scottish weather, with low cloud or a low sun, limits visibility of the way ahead for motorists.
- Ride with a helmet and wear bright and/or reflective clothing to make yourself as visible as possible.
- Always be aware of the traffic in front and behind you, and ride in a road position where you can see and be seen.
- On single track roads, use the passing places to permit vehicles to overtake you safely. Do not delay other road users unnecessarily.
- When stopping at the roadside, only do so in a safe place, away from blind bends and hill crests, where there is better all-round visibility.
- Use bike lights in bad weather or poor light.
- Ensure your bike is roadworthy and carry a basic emergency repair kit.
- Know the Highway Code for cyclists.

Leave no trace

However you are experiencing the fabulous Scottish countryside, it is vital to leave no trace of your visit so that future generations can enjoy the North Coast 500. Take your litter with you and dispose of it responsibly.

- If there are no bins, or the bins are full, do not leave your rubbish at the roadside or by the bins. Take it away with you for later disposal.
- Recycle where possible.
- If you have pets, use a bag to pick up any waste and dispose of it in an appropriate bin.

Camping

Wherever possible, use a designated campsite, and benefit from the on-site facilities. If you do 'wild camp' then this comes with additional responsibilities:

- In Scotland, access rights extend to wild camping. This is light-weight camping, for individuals or a small number of people and for one or two nights only in any one place.
- Avoid wild camping in enclosed fields where there are crops or livestock.
- Keep well away from buildings, roads and historic structures.
- Be mindful of the deer stalking and grouse shooting seasons.
- Always use a camping stove rather than light a fire.
- Do not cause pollution:
  If you need to urinate, do so 100 feet/30 metres from rivers or open water.
  If you need to defecate, do so as far as possible away from buildings, water and livestock. Take a trowel and bury faeces in a shallow hole and replace the turf.
- Take all your rubbish away with you.
- Leave no trace of your camp.

THE SCOTTISH OUTDOOR ACCESS CODE

1. Take responsibility for your own actions.
2. Respect people's privacy and peace of mind.
3. Help land managers and others to work safely and effectively.
4. Care for your environment.
5. Keep your dog under proper control.
6. Take extra care if you are organising an event or running a business and ask the landowner's advice.

For more information and guidance visit: www.outdooraccess-scotland.scot